GROWING DEEPER

DISCIPLE-MAKING LESSONS FOR LIVING AS A FOLLOWER OF JESUS

JONATHAN GALLO

GROWING DEEPER

2ND EDITION

Disciple-Making Lessons for Living as a Follower of Jesus

Jonathan Gallo

GrowingDeeper.us

ISBN 979-8-9890753-0-0 (paperback)

ISBN 979-8-9890753-1-7 (e-book)

Available in paperback and e-book.

Published by

Fill LLC

1317 Edgewater Dr #838

Orlando FL 32804

Edited by: Kerry Wilson, Cover & Layout Design by the Sunday Supply Co.

Dedicated to my wife, Gina, my greatest encourager

CONTENTS:

OTHERS

THEOLOGY

BIBLE STORYLINE

YOUR NEXT STEP

WELCOME

If you have taken the first step to become a follower of Jesus, you've begun one of life's most rewarding journeys! You're about to discover a whole new world and grow daily in your understanding of who God is, who He has created you to be, and all He has planned for you.

Did you know that each day, hundreds of people come to recognize who Jesus is and what He's done? They take a step of faith toward Him, dedicating their lives to serving Him.

The purpose of this book is to guide you as you begin this journey by walking you through some of the essential keys to help you grow and mature into a fully developed follower of Jesus.

HOW DO I USE THIS GUIDE?

In the same way that each of our paths toward Jesus is different, each of our relationships with Christ will look different. We all don't have the same questions, perceptions, assumptions, needs, and dreams. For that reason, there's no perfect way to go through this guide. While each lesson builds on the previous one and connects to future lessons, they can also be taught individually or in a different order. As an example, some people prefer to go through the theology and Bible storyline chapters first, especially if they have questions about the Bible and why it's to be seen as fully true.

While you might want to go through this guide alone, it was designed for mentoring relationships. That means you'll get the fullest experience as you walk with someone who can explain these ideas with you.

It's also essential to recognize that this guide is only the beginning. It summarizes key ideas and concepts as a launching pad for further discussion and teaching found in additional resources referred to you by your mentor.

GROUPS

A typical approach is to pair a mentor with a group of three or four people. Groups operate best when men mentor men, and women mentor women.

While each group is different, most groups will take around forty weeks to complete a full cycle. If your group meets each week, it's possible to finish in under thirty weeks. However, it's normal for a group to spread some lessons over two or three weeks and not to meet over the holidays. For example, if you begin in mid-September, you could finish as early as May.

CLASS

Some churches decide to use part or all of the materials in a class format. Classes are a great way to teach the content. Beyond this, a mentor-mentee relationship creates a unique dynamic that helps to open up an appropriate conversation and better see the application of the ideas.

HOW IS THIS BOOK ORGANIZED?

This book is divided into several parts.

STARTING OUT

In this section, we unpack the main message, baptism, and God's Spirit at work as we begin this journey as followers of Jesus.

GOD

In this section, we focus on how you grow in your relationship with God through quiet time, prayer, reading the Bible, and studying the Bible.

YOU

In this section, we focus on your new identity in Christ, overcoming evil, finding healing, making wise choices, and handling money.

OTHERS

In this section, we focus on how to grow in our relationships with others in our life and in the church. We also look at relationships with people in whom God want us to invest.

THEOLOGY

In this section, we discover some of the foundational lessons for our faith: The Bible, God, Angels & Demons, Realms, Humanity, Sin, Salvation.

BIBLE STORYLINE

In this section, we unpack the Bible's outline through five main sections: Beginnings, Israel, Jesus, Church, and the Future

My prayer is that these lessons don't merely fill your mind with knowledge but that they also help you experience all that Jesus has promised to those who follow Him.

Jonathan Gallo

STARTING OUT

You are invited to a new life.
To a life you have always wanted.
A life of purpose. A life of meaning.
A life that can only be experienced as you stop
trying to live your way.
Come into a relationship with your creator.
Allow Him to show you the big picture and
your part in it.
Let Him lead you, teach you,
and help you along the way,
so that you can be in on all He has planned.

CHAPTER 1

MESSAGE

BIG IDEA

We are invited by Jesus to follow Him.

READING

Matt. 4; John 3

THOUGHTS

Between 25 and 30 AD, Jesus began to travel through ancient Israel, inviting people to follow Him—to leave all they were doing and those they loved to be with Him, to sleep where He slept, to travel where He travelled, and to learn what He taught (Matt. 4:17–22).

Jesus invited the imperfect, sinful, hurting, confused, and rejected. He promised to provide these first followers healing, meaning, and purpose in this life and eternal life after death (Matt. 11:28–30; Mark 2:17; Luke 4:18–21; John 3:16–18, 10:10–11).

As Jesus encountered those who wanted to obtain His prom-ise to them, He emphasized to them that there was only one way to acquire it. They would have to stop believing and living the way they had always believed and lived. They would then have to exclusively follow Him—His way of thinking and way of living (Matt.

10:37–39, 16:24–26; Luke 9:57–62, 18:18–30; John 14:6).

Today, Jesus still invites us to follow and commit our lives to Him. This invitation is centred around four key ideas that serve as a summary of Jesus's message.

1. WE ARE CREATED WITH PURPOSE AND MEANING

God creates us with great purpose and meaning, which can only be fulfilled through a right relationship with Him.

I came so they can have real and eternal life, more and better life than they ever dreamed of. John 10:10

2. SIN DESTROYS

To sin is to try to live independently from God, who is the giver and sustainer of life. As we move away from God, we experience less and less life. When we try to live on our terms, we experience levels of death. We all have sinned. Sin prevents us from experiencing the life God created for us.

All of us, like sheep, have strayed away. We have left God's paths to follow our own. Isa. 53:6

For everyone has sinned; we all fall short of God's glorious way. Rom. 3:23

3. LOVE SAVES

Jesus died to remove the result and power of sin in our lives. He experienced our death for us (Matt. 27:32–56; 1 Tim. 2:3–6).

For the wages of sin is death, but the free gift of God is eternal life through Christ Jesus, our Lord. Rom. 6:23

For God loved the world so much that he gave his one and only Son so that everyone who believes in him will not perish but have eternal life. John 3:16

4. A NEW LIFE AWAITS

Jesus offers us an exchange of His life for our lives. If we give Him our sin and death, He will provide us with His life. That includes the power to live this life now and eternal life after death.

If you confess with your mouth that Jesus is Lord and believe in your heart that God raised him from the dead, you will be saved. It is by believing in your heart that you are made right with God, and it is by confessing with your mouth that you are saved. Rom. 10:9–10

STARTING

The way to get in on this message is to put your faith in Jesus. As you declare to Jesus your commitment to turn from sin and trust Him fully, you begin the journey toward all He has promised (Matt. 10:32; Rom. 10:9–10; 1 John 1:9). Here's a simple prayer you can use to do that.

"Jesus, thank you for loving me. I recognize that I am a sinner. Thank you for dying on the cross for my sin. Today, I ask you to lead my life. I give you control. I surrender my life to you. Amen."

DISCUSSION

Describe times you tried to live life on your terms. What does it mean to move away from dependency on God?

Do you see yourself as a disciple of Jesus?

Discuss with each other your journey of faith and questions that you have about the main message.

Personal Application

CHAPTER NOTES:

_____

_____

_____

_____

_____

_____

_____

_____

_____

_____

_____

_____

_____

_____

_____

_____

_____

_____

See Appendix for Q&A

CHAPTER 2

BAPTISM

If we follow Jesus, we need to get baptized.

Rom. 6:2–10; Col. 2:10–13

Did you know that every religious tradition has cleansing rites to purify and prepare people to approach God? In ancient Judaism, ritual cleansing was a part of everyday religious life. Temple worship required priests to use a ceremonial basin, and washing ceremonies were performed in advance of significant festivals (Exod. 30:17–21).

When we first open the New Testament, we see in Matthew 3 a man named John urging people to turn to God and start living right (v. 2). People are baptized to declare their intention to live in a pure way. Jesus participates in the Jewish symbol of purification (vv. 13–17). Yet as He begins to travel and teach, He changes the idea of this rite. Jesus's message was that He would personally purify us if we place our faith in Him. Baptism became a symbol of faith in Jesus, who makes us pure, rather than a symbol of something we were going to try to do for ourselves.

If you have decided to put your faith in Jesus, it's time to be baptized (Mark 16:16). Jesus taught that baptism is the first step in following Him.

> And He told them, "Go into all the world and preach the Good News to everyone. Anyone who believes and is baptized will be saved." Mark 16:15

BAPTISM IS AN OUTWARD DEMONSTRATION OF AN INWARD DECISION

The word "baptize" comes from the koine Greek word "baptizo." It describes the change that happens as something is immersed in something else, such as dyeing clothes in water or pickling vegetables in vinegar.

Jesus's message was that He would personally change us if we place our faith in Him. Baptism communicates that you have fully immersed yourself in Jesus and that you are being changed from the inside out.

BAPTISM IS IDENTIFICATION WITH JESUS

When you are baptized, you enter into Jesus's death, burial, and resurrection (Rom. 6:2–10; Col. 2:10–13). As you enter the waters, you identify with His death as you die to your old life. As you are submerged in water, you identify with His burial and show that sin no longer has power over you. As you come up out of the water, you identify with His resurrection and the authority Jesus gives you to live a new life. Baptism is a powerful moment you will always remember (1 Pet. 3:21).

BAPTISM IS A CHOICE

While some parents practise infant baptism, Jesus spoke about a different kind of baptism. Jesus's style of baptism was for willing people who had made the personal decision to follow Him.

As we are baptized, we come to take the first step in demonstrating to God, ourselves, and the world that we have chosen to stop living on our terms and live surrendered to God.

You can read more in the following stories: Philip baptizing new converts (Acts 8:12), Philip baptizing the Ethiopian eunuch (Acts 8:35–38), Saul being baptized (Acts 9:17–18), and the baptism of the jailor (Acts 16:30–33), the Jewish synagogue ruler (Acts 18:8), and the believers in Ephesus (Acts 19:4–6).

DISCUSSION

Explain in your own words how baptism is an identification with Jesus's death, burial, and resurrection.

Discuss with each other the moment you were baptized. If you haven't been baptized, discuss what is holding you back.

Personal Application

CHAPTER NOTES:

See Appendix for Q&A

CHAPTER 3

SPIRIT

BIG IDEA

God's Spirit changes everything.

READING

Acts 2; 1 Pet. 1 & 2

THOUGHTS

Inside

The moment you put your faith in Jesus, God sends His Spirit to live in you. This is God's promise to you (Ezek. 36:27; Rom. 8:9; 1 Cor. 6:19–20).

Each of you must repent of your sins and turn to God, and be baptized in the name of Jesus Christ for the forgiveness of your sins. Then you will receive the gift of the Holy Spirit. Acts 2:38–39

Born

When God's Spirit comes to live in you, your spirit comes alive. This is called spiritual birth, or being "born again." This is the start of a new life (John 3:3–7; 1 Pet. 1:23).

It is by his great mercy that we have been born again. 1 Pet. 1:3

Connect

The Spirit connects you to God. Through the Spirit, all God is and all He offers become available directly to you (Gal. 4:6; 1 John 2:27).

For he raised us from the dead along with Christ and seated us with him in the heavenly realms because we are united with Christ Jesus. Eph. 2:6

Filled

As we read God's Word, spend time with Him in prayer, listen to His nudging, share our faith, and do what He calls us to do, the Spirit continues to fill us with Himself. We are to surrender to God and seek to be continually filled by the Spirit. Over time you will notice yourself challenged to let your weakness and vice be fully controlled by God (John 15:1–17; Acts 4:29–31).

Be filled with the Holy Spirit. Eph. 5:18–19

Change

The Spirit is working to grow and change us to be like Jesus (1 John 3:2) with new thoughts and perspectives (Rom. 12:2; Eph. 4:23–25), new attitudes and motivations (Phil. 2:5–8; 1 Tim. 1:5), and new habits and behaviours (Matt. 6:33; Gal. 5:22). The result of this work is a greater love for God, yourself, and others (Rom. 5:5; Eph. 3:19).

So all of us can see and reflect the image of Jesus who makes us more and more like him as we are changed into his image. 2 Cor. 3:16

Fruit

The Spirit always leads us in the direction that reflects and produces the character and nature of God. This is called the fruit of the Spirit.

But the Holy Spirit produces this kind of fruit in our lives: love, joy, peace, patience, kindness, goodness, faithfulness, gentleness, and self-control. There is no law against these things! Gal. 5:22

Gifts

God wants to use us in the lives of others. The Spirit will put a desire in you to serve others in your world in unique ways. This spiritual lens is how God has positioned you to impact others inside and outside the church. The Spirit makes you a gift to the world: at home, in your community, and in your vocation.

We learn that there are ministry (functional) gifts, such as apostles, prophets, evangelists, pastors, and teachers (Eph. 4:11), and motivational (practical) gifts such as service, exhortation, giving, leadership, mercy, helps, and administration (Rom. 12:3–7). See the Appendix for an explanation of each of these gifts.

Power

The Spirit also wants to work through us in powerful ways. As we pray for the Spirit to completely immerse us, we will see His power overflow through us as we reach out to serve others (Acts 2:2–12; 1 Cor. 12:1–12, 28).

As the Spirit empowers us, we will flow in gifts of wisdom, knowledge, discernment, prophecy, tongues, interpretation, faith, healing, and miracles. See the Appendix for an explanation of each of these gifts in greater detail.

Sometimes the process of first seeing these extra ordinary gifts flow through us is called "Spirit Baptism." We see in Acts a pattern of people experiencing the power of the Spirit through persistent personal prayer (Acts 2) and having someone pray for them who has already experienced God's Spirit in these ways (Acts 8:17, 19:1–6; 2 Tim. 1:6). In the early church, it was normative to see tongues expressed first as a sign of Spirit Baptism (Acts 2, 8, 9, 10, 11 , 19; Rom. 8:26, 27; 1 Cor. 14:22).

Guide

The Spirit inside you reminds you of things that God has said in the Bible. The Spirit will give you an inner nudge to challenge you to make the right choices. As you respond to that nudge, you will become more and more aware of the Spirit speaking into your life (John 14:26, 16:7–15).

When the Spirit of truth comes, he will guide you into all truth. John 16:13

Eternity

The Spirit is preparing us for life after this life. We have much to look forward to in eternity (1 Cor. 15; 1 John 5).

Now we live with high expectation ... and through your faith, God is protecting you by his power until you receive this salvation, which is ready to be revealed on the last day for all to see. 1 Pet. 1:3–5

In the following sections, you will discover your part in allowing God's Spirit to work in your life as you learn to love God, yourself, and others. Ask the Spirit of God to baptize you and work supernaturally through you. Ask someone who has experienced the baptism of the Spirit to pray for you.

DISCUSSION

What changes have you noticed in your life since you decided to follow Jesus?

Do you realize it is the Spirit at work in your life? Do you sense inner nudges from God?

Explain the difference between the moment the Spirit comes to live in you and Spirit Baptism.

Personal Application

CHAPTER NOTES:

See Appendix for Q&A

GOD

Jesus replied, "'You must love the Lord your God with all your heart, all your soul, and all your mind. This is the first and greatest commandment." **Matt. 22:37–39**

CHAPTER 4

QUIET TIME

We build a relationship with God by intentionally connecting with Him each day.

Adam and Eve—Gen. 3:8; Enoch—Gen. 5:22–24; Abraham—Gen. 17:1; Isaac—Gen. 26:24; Jacob—Gen. 35:9; Noah—Gen. 6:13; Moses—Exod. 24:12-13; Samuel—1 Sam. 3:10; David—Ps. 5:3; Isaiah—Isa. 50:4.

Our relationship with God grows through regular connections. The example that we have from Jesus is that He spent time alone, away from the busyness of the day to be with God (Mark 1:35; Luke 5:15–16).

As you pursue moments of connection with God, you'll find that they will help you gain spiritual strength (Matt. 4:4b) and will provide direction and wisdom for each day (Ps. 32:8, 119:105).

You can spend time anywhere that helps you connect to God. Some people dedicate space at home. Others use headphones as they travel by bus or subway to work. Still others spend time with God as they walk through the forest or by the ocean. Wherever you choose, God is the focus. There are a variety of elements that you can make part of your connection with God.

Prayer

Prayer is talking with God. It's a conversation that might seem challenging to start but is one of the most rewarding experiences you can have. In the next section, we'll spend some time unpacking the various ways you can learn to pray.

The Bible.

Quiet time includes reading the Bible. The Bible is a record of God's interaction with people in history. These conversations are recorded for us to glean more about His character, nature, purpose, and thoughts. As you begin reading, you'll find your ideas challenged and will start to learn more about who God is and His plan for your life. The Bible is like spiritual food to help fill you on the inside.

Music

Music is an emotional language that can help us get our minds focused on who God is and what He has or can do in our life. Getting a playlist of instrumental or worship music can help drown out the noise of the world around us and better get into a concentrated space. We can also connect with God when we sing to God from our hearts (Col. 3:13–16; Eph. 5:19).

Art

Some individuals like to take a verse from the Bible and illustrate it. It's a way of bringing the thought or idea to life.

Journaling

Writing down the things you're thinking, praying about, pondering on, or learning is a great way to summarize and remember your experience later. Some people like to write down their thoughts in a journal, and others use apps.

Communion

You can take time to remember Jesus's suffering, death, and resurrection in as found in 1 Corinthians 11:23–26.

Retreats

Some people like to go on prolonged weekend retreats of silence to quiet the noise of life and increase their awareness and hearing of God.

Spiritual Conversations

We can connect with God along with other people. Sometimes reading the Bible with someone else and discussing your perspective can help you connect with God (Acts 2:42–44).

Serving

We can connect with God as we serve other people as if we were serving Jesus (Matt. 25:40).

Quiet Time Example—Here Is an Example of Quiet Time

- Talk to God (2 min.): "God, I invite you into my day. Speak to me today. I want to hear from you, and I want to know you more. I need you in every part of my life."

- Read the Bible (5-10 min.): Read a little bit at a time. Often, less is more. By reading a shorter amount and going over it a few times, you'll get the sense of what it's saying.

- Listen and write down your thoughts (5 min.): It's great to come out of each moment with a thought and then use a journal or app to record the ideas or questions raised by what you just read.

- Talk to God (5 min.): Finish off by merely talking out of your heart to God. Express. Confess. Question. Give thanks. Ask.

Intentionality

Setting down quality time with God is not something that happens unless you make it a priority. If you've never done it, start with as little as ten minutes a day. Don't get down on yourself if you miss a day. Remember, it's a lifestyle change that takes time to develop.

If you've never developed the rhythm and habit of prayer and quiet time, it's often useful to buddy up with someone you can weekly debrief on your progress. It can be done in person, online, or over the phone. It's a great way to develop a habit. A relationship grows with time. Use the journal in the Appendix to track your daily quiet time.

CHAPTER NOTES:

See Appendix for Q&A

DISCUSSION

What distractions generally come up when you intend to have a regular connection with God?

_____

_____

_____

Describe the mindset shift that is needed to see quiet time motivated out of obligation to love.

_____

_____

_____

Personal Application

_____

_____

_____

_____

_____

_____

_____

_____

_____

CHAPTER 5

PRAYER

BIG IDEA

Prayer is as simple as talking to God.

READING

Matt. 6:5–18

THOUGHTS

Many people get stuck because of their misconceptions of prayer. They feel that they need to use particular words. They think that there's a specific way to pray. They believe that one must come up with a great sounding prayer to be heard by God. They feel guilty after days of not talking to God.

Prayer is part of the relationship. It's what you do out of love, not out of obligation. Prayer is talking with God. It's speaking, and it's listening. We learn that it needs to flow from our heart (Ps. 18:6; Mark 15:34), simply (Matt. 6:7), honestly, authentically (Ps. 38:9; Prov. 16:2; James 4:3), and humbly (2 Chron. 7:14; Ps. 66:18).

As we talk to God, we learn that prayer is not for God's benefit; it's for ours. We find several benefits as we speak with God regularly.

- We develop a close relationship with God (Matt. 6:5–13; John 17:11, 20–21).

- We are filled with peace (Phil. 4:6–7).

- We are strengthened to fight temptation (Matt. 26:1).

- We are encouraged when we are tired (Luke 18:1).

- We are prepared to hear God's voice (John 14:26).

- We are ready to receive His wisdom (James 1:5).

- We are positioned to have our needs supplied (Matt. 7:7,8; John 16:24).

Types of Prayer

Jesus modelled many kinds of ways of talking with God (Matt. 6:5–13; Luke 18:1; John 17; Eph. 6:18). He promised that God hears us each time we pray, and He knows what we need before we ask (Matt. 6:7–8).

- Pre-scripted—Jesus prayed the psalms and modelled prayer (Ps. 22:1, 31:5).

- Spontaneous—Jesus modelled prayer from the heart (John 17).

- Praise or Adoration—We recognize God for who He is (Matt. 11:25).

- Thanksgiving—We thank God for what He has done (John 11:41).

- Petition—We pray for needs and wisdom (Heb. 5:7).

- Agreement—We pray God's will as revealed in His Word

- (Acts 4:23–24).

- Intercession—We pray for others (Luke 22:32; John 17).

- Listening—We wait to hear God speaking to us, and we can listen to His Spirit talk to us in a personal way (1 Kings 19:11–12).

A Model Prayer

Jesus gave us a model prayer as a way of teaching His disciples to pray spontaneously out of their hearts. We can learn to talk to God in the same way. As you follow each section, you can start to put the parts into your own words.

"Our Father in heaven, hallowed be your name, your kingdom come, your will be done on earth as it is in heaven. Give us today our daily bread. Forgive us our debts, as we also have forgiven our debtors. And lead us not into temptation, but deliver us from the evil one, for yours is the kingdom and the power and the glory forever." Matt. 6:9–13

"Our Father in heaven ..."
God wants to be known as our Father (Rom. 8:15). Thank Him for the relationship you have with Him.

"... Hallowed be Your Name ..."
Recognize who God is in your life. Saviour. Healer. Provider. Peace. Thank Him for all He has done for you.

"... Your Kingdom come, Your will be done on earth as it is in heaven..."
Submit your life and agenda to God's priorities. Give the situations in your life to Him to take care of His way.

"... Give us this day, our daily bread ..."
Ask Him for your daily needs. Let Him know your needs and depend on Him for the results.

"... Forgive us our debts as we forgive our debtors ..."
Ask God to forgive you of your sin. Talk to God about the pain

others have brought to you. Forgive them, and release them from owing you in any way.

"... And do not lead us into temptation but deliver us from the evil one..."
Pray that God helps you resist temptations that come from inside you and from outside of you (Eph. 6:12).

"... For yours is the Kingdom and the Power and the Glory forever."
Express your faith in God's ability to accomplish His plan and purpose ultimately.

DISCUSSION

What did you learn about prayer in this section?

What hinders you from praying regularly?

Do you think there is a unique way to pray?

Personal Application

CHAPTER NOTES:

See Appendix for Q&A

CHAPTER 6

READING THE BIBLE

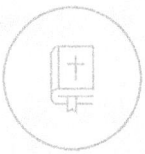

Reading the Bible is essential to growing in faith.

Ps. 1; Ps. 19

As we will discover in the theology section, the Bible is God's view of the world, collected for us. This is important because life is filled with voices that tell us what to believe and how to live. As we read the Bible in our quiet time, we get to know who God is, how He works, and how we can live a better life. When we begin applying what we read, we begin to experience the promised results: inner peace and freedom, wisdom and understanding, and so much more. This builds our trust in God, and the cycle of growth continues (Ps. 1, 19:7–11, 119:97–105; Rom. 12:1–2; 1 Pet. 1:23–25).

Reading the Bible

Several tools can help you read the Bible. You can follow along with a reading plan, listen to an audio version, or just read it as you would a book. A Bible reading plan is included in the Appendix. It's compiled from fifty important passages in the Bible that will help you read through the main storyline.

Contemplating the Bible

As we spend focused time thinking through one passage that we read in the Bible, we can gain unique insights that transform our lives.

As an example, write down one or two passages of scripture and look at that scripture over a few days. As you focus, write all the ideas that come to your mind as a result.

But they delight in the law of the LORD, meditating on it day and night. Ps. 1

Memorizing

As you invest time memorizing scripture, you'll see that at key moments in your life, those verses will come back to you. Start with short passages and work your way up to more substantial chapters.

I have hidden your word in my heart that I might not sin against you. Ps. 119:11

Studying

It's possible to go deeper in your understanding of the Bible by learning to study the Bible. See the section on studying the Bible.

And the people of Berea were more open-minded than those in Thessalonica, and they listened eagerly to Paul's message. They searched the Scriptures day after day to see if Paul and Silas were teaching the truth. Acts 17:11

DISCUSSION

How are you generally discouraged from reading the Bible?

Personal Application

CHAPTER NOTES:

See Appendix for Q&A

CHAPTER 7

STUDYING THE BIBLE

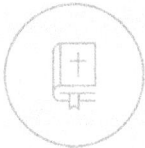

We can learn to study the Bible.

2 Tim. 3:14–4:4; Heb. 4:12

As we have learned, God speaks to us as we spend time reading the Bible. As we invest time studying the Bible, we can grow deeper in our understanding and love for God. Proper hermeneutics (how to interpret the Bible) can be summarized in three steps: seeing, understanding, and applying.

Seeing

The entire purpose of this first step is to observe all that is happening. Read through the entire passage a few times. As you do, try to answer the following questions: Who are the characters? What is happening? When is it happening? Where is it happening? Why is it happening? Circle words or concepts that are confusing that you would like to understand better. You can also outline the chapter to help you get a better sense of what is happening.

Understanding

The second step is to understand what you have come to observe by putting it into context. There are various ways to understand the original intention of what was written before applying it to our present situation.

- Placement: How does the passage apply within the context of the greater story that it's in? Verse > Paragraph > Section > Book > Era > Bible > God (eternal)

- History & Culture: What is the culture and history of the period in which the passage is written? What does the passage say and not say? What do outside sources help us understand about the culture?

- Literary: What type of literature am I reading? Is it biographical, apocalyptic, exposition, narrative, parable, poetry, poetry, proverb, satire, wisdom? Is it meant to be factual, symbolic, or metaphorical? Is it personally reflective or directive?

- Theological: How does it compare to other passages? Is it consistent? Is it the only place where the idea is found in the Bible? Is there a paradox that I don't understand?

- Spiritual: Are there layers of understanding in the passage? Can it refer to multiple ideas?

- Jesus: How does this scripture reveal Jesus? How does it fit into the life and message of Jesus (Heb. 1:1–2)?

Outside Resources

You can use external resources to help you find out more about what's happening in the passage you're reading. Start by studying the words that you circled and referring to outside commentaries on the chapters themselves to understand the context behind what you are considering.

- Bible Dictionary—This is a tool that helps summarize the meanings of difficult Bible words. Some of the most popular are the Vines Bible Dictionary and Easton's Bible Dictionary.

- Commentaries—These provide an explanation of a passage of scripture based on the author's understanding and knowledge. Some of the most popular ones were written by Matthew Henry, John Gill, Jamieson Fausset and Brown, and the Expositors.

- Concordance/Lexicon—This tool helps you understand the original language for each translated word.

- Online—Many of these tools are found for free online at Bible Gateway, Biblestudytools.com, and Bible.com.

- Software—You can also find software that combines all of the above at e-sword.net, olivetree.com, logos.com

Applying

The final step is to make the principles practically relevant. Here are a few ways you can take what you have read and understand how it applies today. As you work with a mentor, you'll be able to use the scripture in your situation in a healthy way and apply it to life situations on your own.

- Categorize the timeless truth (principles): What does this passage suggest about all times and all places? About God, human nature, society?

- Find contemporary parallels: In what types of situations do I find a similar principle working today?

- What don't I understand ? What is unclear and hard to

understand? What do I need more help with or need to leave alone rather than conclude currently?

- Spiritual application: Is there a personal message to me from God? Does the passage spark ideas or thoughts as I journal and begin to hear God for myself?

- Confronting our thoughts: How does this principle contradict my ideas about life and God? What would I have customarily believed to be true? Who will I trust: my thoughts and experiences, or what God teaches? What does this mean about how I interpret the past? What does this suggest about how I live my life? What do I have to change?

With the help of your mentor, try applying these principles to a passage such as 1 Sam. 3:1–10. What are the timeless truths that you pull out of these verses?

PERSONAL APPLICATION

_____

_____

_____

_____

_____

_____

_____

_____

_____

CHAPTER NOTES:

See Appendix for Q&A

YOU

"Love your neighbour as yourself" **Matt. 22:39**

CHAPTER 8

IDENTITY

You have a new identity.

Eph. 1, 2

As we grow as Jesus followers, we become more and more aware of our new identity. We no longer identify with our past. We begin to identify with who we are and who we are becoming.

As a result of Jesus's death, burial, and resurrection, God sees you differently too. You will notice in the New Testament verses that talk about all we have because we are "in Christ." As you follow Jesus, you'll discover all that this entails (John 15; Eph. 1–2; Col. 3:3–4).

Anyone who belongs to Christ has become a new person. The old life is gone; a new life has begun! 2 Cor. 5:17

God Is Your True and Perfect Father

When you picture God, what do you see? Do you see an old man with a long beard sitting on a throne? Do you see someone who is angry, wanting to punish you? As you walk with God, you will begin to see Him as He really is. He's unlike famous mythical figures. He's unlike our earthly parental examples. He's the best example of a father you could imagine (John 14:6–21, 20:17; James 1:17).

> And because we are his children, God has sent the Spirit of his Son into our hearts, prompting us to call out, "Abba, Father." Now you are no longer a slave but God's own child. And since you are his child, God has made you his heir. Gal. 4:6–7

HERE ARE A FEW BENEFITS FOR BEING "IN CHRIST."

A Child of God

When you come to faith, you are spiritually reborn as God's son/daughter. You become a child of God. This changes everything about you (John 3:3–6; Rom. 8:9, 15; Gal. 3:26; 1 John 3:1–3).

> Yet to all who did receive him, to those who believed in his name, he gave the right to become children of God—children born not of natural descent, nor of human decision or a husband's will, but born of God. John 1:12–13

Loved

God's love for you always was and always will be unconditional. It's not based on performance or behaviour. It's based on His character and nature (John 3:16; Rom. 5:5, 8, 8:37–39; 1 John 4:7–11).

> See how very much our Father loves us, for he calls us his children, and that is what we are! 1 John 3:1

Forgiven

You are totally and completely forgiven. God doesn't hold your sin, no matter how terrible, against you. You are free from the power and consequences of sin (Eph. 1:7; Col. 1:13–14, 2:13–15; 1 John 1:9).

There is no condemnation for those who belong to Christ Jesus. Rom. 8:1

Others

A few other markers of our new identity include: uncondemned (Rom. 8:1), set free (Rom. 8:2,33), pure (1 Cor. 1:2), justified (Gal. 2:16); blessed (Eph. 1:4), recreated (Eph. 2:10), empowered (Phil. 4:13), friends of God (John 15:15), and heirs of salvation (Heb. 1:14).

DISCUSSION

In your own words, describe your new identity.

_____

_____

_____

_____

How does your new identity change how you begin to see yourself?

_____

_____

_____

Personal Application

_____

_____

_____

_____

_____

_____

_____

_____

_____

_____

CHAPTER NOTES:

_____

_____

_____

_____

_____

_____

_____

_____

_____

_____

_____

_____

_____

_____

_____

_____

_____

_____

See Appendix for Q&A

CHAPTER 9

PURPOSE

God created us with purpose.

God has created us all with purpose. As you'll see in the "Humanity" teaching in the theology section, God created us in His image to reflect Him in our world (Gen. 1:26–28). This develops into four general applications for each person.

Relationship with God

We are created to walk with our creator. We have spent considerable time in previous chapters discussing this and teaching how one can grow in their relationship with God.

Human Relationships

We are created to experience fulfilling human relationships. These relationships can be found in the context of family and friendships. We will spend some time talking about this in the next section on "Others."

It is not good that humanity is alone. Gen. 2:18

Spreading the Good News

We have a purpose in joining God in His mission to restore this world through disciple-making. We will talk more about this in the section on "Sharing your Story" and "Disciple-Making."

Therefore, go and make disciples of all the nations ... Matt. 28:18

Helping Make This World Better

We are all given talents and abilities to make this world a better place. We need to discover them and use them to the best of our ability. This includes our spiritual gifts, personalities, aptitudes, and past experiences.

Then God blessed them and said, "Be fruitful and multiply. Fill the earth and govern it. Reign over it ... Gen. 1:28

Spiritual Gifts

When we put our faith in Jesus, God gives spiritual gifts to every believer. These gifts are often strongly related to our pre-faith talents and abilities, but they don't have to be. Three useful tests for discerning a spiritual gift are: you enjoy it, you are effective in it, and other people confirm it's a gift God works through you. You can find out more about spiritual gifts in the section on the "Holy Spirit." You can find different spiritual gift tests online to help you discover yours.

Personalities

God loves variety. He makes us all unique and gives us a personal style. We each relate to others, take in information, make decisions, and structure our lives differently. Many different personality tests can help you grow in understanding how you are and how you might lean.

Aptitudes

Each of us has different abilities. Some are more artistic than others. Some of us are better with words and some better with numbers. There are many aptitudes and career tests that can help you identify what you're good at doing. Sometimes what we take for granted in ourselves is a unique way that God created us and part of our purpose in our world.

Experiences

God can turn our past experiences for good. He can take past work experiences, relationship experiences, and life experiences to make us wise and to help other people.

Awareness

As you become aware of how God created you individually, you will more fully appreciate His design for your life. As you invest your unique gifting in others, you'll understand how you are created to contribute to our world.

DISCUSSION

What are your spiritual gifts?

_____

_____

_____

_____

How do your personality, aptitudes, and experiences shape your role in making our world better?

_____

_____

_____

_____

Personal Application

_____

_____

_____

_____

_____

_____

_____

_____

_____

_____

_____

CHAPTER NOTES:

_____

_____

_____

_____

_____

_____

_____

_____

_____

_____

_____

_____

_____

_____

_____

See Appendix for Q&A

CHAPTER 10

OVERCOMING EVIL

BIG IDEA

We can be part of overcoming evil in our world.

READING

Rom. 8

THOUGHTS

We live in a world filled with pain and evil. All the evil and brokenness in the world is a result of sin. As we move away from reflecting God, we experience less and less life—or more and more death. Sin destroys us, our relationships, and our world (Rom. 6:23, 8:20–21).

Sin

As we will discuss in more detail in the theology section, to sin is to live independently from God, who is the source of all life. Sin can be an attitude, thought, or behaviour that doesn't reflect God's character and nature. The Bible articulates what sin looks like (Exod. 20; 1 Cor. 6:9–10; Gal. 5:19–21; Eph. 5:3–7; 1 Tim. 1:9–10). All of us have the propensity to sin (Ps. 14:3; Rom. 3:23; 1 John 1:8).

When you follow the desires of your sinful nature, the results are obvious: sexual immorality, impurity, lustful pleasures, idolatry, sorcery, hostility, quarrelling, jealousy, outbursts of anger, selfish ambition, dissension, division, envy, drunkenness, wild parties, and other sins like these. Gal. 5:19–21

Spiritual

There is a spiritual force of evil that also wants to get us to reject God's work and authority in our life. In chapters 20-21, we talk through the spiritual world and demons in more detail (John 10:10; 1 Pet. 5:8; 1 John 5:19).

For we are not fighting against flesh-and-blood enemies, but against evil rulers and authorities of the unseen world, against mighty powers in this dark world, and against evil spirits in the heavenly places. Eph. 6:12

Temptation

Followers of Jesus are not immune to the temptation of sin. There is influence found in the world, from others, and the old life in us (1 Tim. 6:9; James 1:13–15; 1 John 2:15–17).

One day Jesus said to his disciples, "There will always be temptations to sin …" Luke 17:1

Battle

God's Spirit battles against the old life in us that wants to lead us into sin. We prepare for the temptations and fight against the desires as we read God's Word, pray, listen to the nudges of the Spirit, and employ spiritual armour. If we experience a moment of failure, it's not over; we can step up again to fight (Ps. 119:11; Rom. 6:12–14, 8:1–9, 26–27; Eph. 6:10–18; James 4:7).

The temptations in your life are no different from what others experience. And God is faithful. He will not allow the temptation to be more than you can stand. When you are tempted, he will show you a way out so that you can endure. 1 Cor. 10:13

Repentance

Not only is repentance the first step in following Jesus, but it's a daily activity/response when we give in to temptation (Acts 2:38, 3:19, 5:31, 11:18, 17:30). Repentance means: to completely turn, to stop, pivot, and walk in another direction. Repentance is a decision to stop trusting self and to leave sinful thinking and living behind.

Receive Grace

We must remember that all we have is a result of what Jesus has done and offered freely to those who make Him Lord of their life. This is called grace, and it's a gift of forgiveness that can't be earned (John 1:14–17; Rom. 3:20–27, 5:17; 2 Cor. 8:9; Eph. 2:8–9; Heb. 2:9).

Faith

The next part of repentance is to trust Jesus fully. This is called faith and refers to both our attitude and actions. When we embrace right living (1 Cor. 6:9–11; Gal. 5:19–21; Titus 2:11–14; Heb. 12:14) and trust God despite circumstances (Heb. 10:38–11:5) it grows deeper every day (2 Cor. 5:7; 2 Tim. 4:7). Faith is what God is ultimately looking for from us (Luke 18:8; Heb. 11:6).

When troubles of any kind come your way, consider it an opportunity for great joy. For you know that when your faith is tested, your endurance has a chance to grow. So let it grow, for when your endurance is fully developed, you will be perfect and complete, needing nothing. James 1:2–4

Lordship

A "Lord" is one who has total authority and power over a realm of influence. Another way to articulate the steps of repentance and faith is to say that we must make Jesus our Lord. It's the acknowledgment that everything in the world is created and ruled by Jesus (2 Chron. 20:6; Col. 1:16), that God has elevated Jesus as Lord of all (Acts 2:36, 17:24; Eph. 1:18–22), that one day everyone will recognize Jesus as Lord (Rom. 14:11–12; Phil. 2:5–11; 2 Thess. 1:7–9), and that Jesus wants us to make Him our Lord today and each day voluntarily (Acts 17:30–31; Rom. 14:9).

Advance

We can fight evil in the world by living in Jesus's way, overcoming evil with God's love, and inviting people to follow Jesus (Luke 6:27–38; Rom. 12:14–21; 1 John 5:4).

Don't let evil conquer you, but conquer evil by doing good.
Rom. 12:21

DISCUSSION

Read the list of sins in Galatians 5:19–21. What did you never consider to be sin before reading this?

_____

_____

_____

What are some examples of temptations you face?

_____

_____

_____

What are some ways you can resist evil?

_____

_____

_____

Personal Application

_____

_____

_____

_____

_____

CHAPTER NOTES:

See Appendix for Q&A

CHAPTER 11

HEALING

BIG IDEA

God wants to heal our emotions, our minds, and our bodies. He also wants to use us to bring healing to our world.

READING

James 5:13–20

THOUGHTS

Broken

As we have already discovered, when we walk away from God (life's source), we embrace different levels of death. This turning away from God is called sin. As a result, we experience brokenness in our society. Sin affects our physical bodies and our souls— the way we think, our emotions, and our desires (Ps. 51; Isa. 53:6; Rom. 6:23).

Re-creation

God is re-creating our world and removing sin and death. We

are promised a future with new physical bodies unaffected by sickness and disease (Rev. 22).

Healing

We can receive a measure of healing as we wait for the ultimate process of full healing. The Spirit in us can bring a measure of that future reality for us to experience today (Mark 16:17–18).

Physical Healing

While our bodies will ultimately die, we can ask God to temporarily reverse the process of decay (pain and death) in our bodies. Jesus healed many people during His ministry. He encouraged his disciples to heal the sick and seek God for healing (Mark 16:15–18).

Are any of you sick? You should call for the elders of the church to come and pray over you, anointing you with oil in the name of the Lord. Such a prayer offered in faith will heal the sick, and the Lord will make you well. And if you have committed any sins, you will be forgiven. James 5:14–15

Healing of the Mind

As we are open to seeing God's truth replace lies, we will come to believe and will experience personal freedom. This becomes a daily habit that slowly transforms us. What did you once find to be true that you now know to be false? What other beliefs about God, yourself, or others do you think will be challenged?

Don't copy the behaviour and customs of this world, but let God transform you into a new person by changing the way you think. Rom. 12:1–2

Healing of Our Emotions

As we invite the Spirit to heal past hurts, help us to forgive offenders, and release bitterness, we can find emotional freedom. What areas of past hurt do you need God to work on in your life (Matt. 18:21–35; Heb. 12:15)?

He heals the brokenhearted and bandages their wounds. Ps. 147:3

Challenges

As we grow in our relationship with Jesus, read the Bible, pray, and allow Him to heal our mind and emotions, we will be better able to face challenges. Because healing is gradual, we grow stronger each day. We cannot get discouraged if we fail but must continually ask God to help us with whatever we face (Deut. 7:22; Gal. 5:17–24; Eph. 6:10–18; 1 John 2:1–17).

The temptations in your life are no different from what others experience. And God is faithful. He will not allow the temptation to be more than you can stand. When you are tempted, he will show you a way out so that you can endure. 1 Cor. 10:13

The World

God can use us as agents of healing in our world. We can make a difference in our relationships, in our community, and through our vocation. We can invite people to let God work in their own lives and use our influence to see kingdom ideas take shape (2 Cor. 5:11–21; Col. 3:17).

DISCUSSION

Describe the brokenness that you see in the world.

_____

_____

_____

What areas of your life do you need God to bring healing to?

_____

_____

_____

How might God want to use you to bring healing to the world through your vocation?

_____

_____

_____

Personal Application

_____

_____

_____

_____

_____

CHAPTER NOTES:

See Appendix for Q&A

CHAPTER 12

WISE CHOICES

BIG IDEA

You can make wise choices.

READING

Prov. 1

THOUGHTS

We all make decisions differently. Some of us do what feels right or what we think is right, and some of us follow our heart, our gut, or our experience. We all like to make the right decisions that benefit the people we love and ourselves, yet we often make bad decisions. Consider this question for a moment: How do you usually make decisions?

Wisdom

Wisdom is the key to making good choices. As you grow in God-centred wisdom, you will be able to make significant decisions with short- and long-term benefits (Prov. 16:16, 19:8).

Getting wisdom is the wisest thing you can do, and whatever else you do, develop good judgment. Prov. 4:7

Priorities

Wisdom starts by putting God first. It begins with a great love for God and a desire to understand His character and nature. Sometimes the decision to put God first may cost us in the short term, yet putting God first also pays dividends in the long run (Deut. 6:5; Mark 12:30).

Fear of the Lord is the foundation of wisdom. Knowledge of the Holy One results in good judgment. Prov. 9:10

The Bible

The Bible gives us principles for living well. As you read and obey God's Word, you will notice your ability to make wise choices increase. You will see that you will get the results He designed for you to experience (Ps. 19:7–14).

Your word is a lamp to guide my feet and a light for my path. Ps. 119:105

Counsel

We are also encouraged to seek out wisdom from those who are farther along the path than we are. These are advisors who have our best interests in mind and aren't shy about telling us what we need to hear. Who are those you look to for counsel in your life? You might have to pursue people rather than hoping they will appear before you.

Where no counsel is, the people fall: but in the multitude of counsellors, there is safety. Prov. 11:14

Speaking

God also wants to give us personal direction and an inner nudge as to the direction we ought to take in each situation. As we are faithful to obey His Word and His inner nudges, we can become aware of Him speaking to us in different circumstances.

You will hear a voice behind you saying, "This is the way. Follow it, whether it turns to the right or the left." Isa. 30:21

Complexity

There are often moments when we're faced with complex situations in which there are no simple answers. God has promised to give us supernatural wisdom in those situations. If we ask God for wisdom and wait on Him until the answer comes, we can be sure that He will show us the right decision to make. It takes patience and a willingness to trust the process (Isa. 30:21).

If you need wisdom, ask our generous God, and he will give it to you. He will not rebuke you for the asking. James 1:5

Questions

Wisdom can sometimes be found in taking into consideration past experiences, present circumstances, and future dreams. Here are a few questions you can ask as you contemplate future decisions: Does this honour God? Is this the right thing to do? Does this promote human life? Am I acting out of good motives? Is this loving toward God, myself, and other people? How does this reflect my priorities and responsibilities? What will I regret doing/not doing? What are the short- and long-term implications of this decision? Can I afford/not afford this?

Perhaps you need to create a chart with all the positive and negative ramifications of the choices you will make. Writing things down creates clarity. What are a few other questions you might add to this list?

Sovereignty

The bad news is that we're all prone to making bad decisions. We're all growing to understand truth more, to handle our emotions, to be healed from past experiences, and to learn God's perspective. The good news is that when you make bad decisions,

God can still turn bad situations into beautiful endings.

And we know that God causes everything to work together for the good of those who love God and are called according to his purpose for them. Rom. 8:28

DISCUSSION

How can you rest in the fact that despite the decisions you make, God can turn them for your good?

Personal Application

CHAPTER NOTES:

See Appendix for Q&A

CHAPTER 13

MONEY

BIG IDEA

We need to learn how to handle money God's way.

READING

Matt. 6:19–33

THOUGHTS

There are over two thousand references to money in the Bible. It is by far one of the most popular topics. Jesus spent time teaching about money as well. As we grow in faith and spiritual maturity, we'll understand and apply biblical principles to handling finances. Here are some of the principles we find in the Bible.

1. The Way We Handle Money Reflects Our Heart.

Money is a temporary tool for this life. It is neither good nor bad. Yet how we handle it reflects what we truly believe and in whom we trust.

For where your treasure is, there your heart will also be. Matt. 6:19–21

2. All Our Resources Are from God.

When we understand that all we have is given to us by God, we'll see ourselves as managers of resources more than owners of the resources in our care. We need to see our bank accounts as His bank accounts, our investments as His investments, our businesses as His businesses.

It can be hard to give control of the money we've worked to earn over to Jesus. It can be hard to change our savings, investing, giving, and spending habits, especially the ones we're used to and comfortable with. It can be hard to see that what we manage isn't ours but has been given to us.

Yet as we grow in our relationship with God, we're to grow in wisdom in how we handle resources entrusted to us. We're to see them multiplied. We're to see them grow. We're to use them to see our family blessed. We're to use them to see His kingdom advanced (Matt. 6:31–34; Col. 3:17).

No one can serve two masters. For you will hate one and love the other; you will be devoted to one and despise the other. You cannot serve both God and money. Matt. 6:24

3. We Are Designed to Work

God provides us with the strength, wisdom, ability, and capacity to work. We're to choose careers that will help us provide for our families. As we find suitable employment and work hard at it as employees or business owners, we'll see our needs provided for (Gen. 2:15; 2 Thess. 3:10).

He who steals must steal no longer; but rather he must labour, performing with his own hands what is good, so that he will have something to share with one who has need. Eph. 4:28

4. We Are Designed to Grow Financial Capacity.

As we save and make wise investment choices, we'll see God grow our capacity. Greed can trap us. Wisdom will help us look for opportunities that honour God and yield a good return. The love of money can destroy us; however, as we are faithful in a few things, we will grow in our capacity to oversee more (1 Chron. 4:10; Matt. 25:14–27; Luke 14:28; 3 John 1:2).

But you shall remember the LORD your God, for it is He who is giving you the power to make wealth. Deut. 8:18

5. We Are to Be Wise in Our Spending.

As we are wise in our spending, we will see God provide for all our needs. We need to pay our bills, live within our means, get rid of debt, and be disciplined in our spending. We need to be on guard against both materialism and a poverty mentality (Matt. 6:31–34; 2 Pet. 3:10–14).

Instruct those who are rich in this present world not to be conceited or to fix their hope on the uncertainty of riches, but on God, who richly supplies us with all things to enjoy. Instruct them to do good, to be rich in good works, to be generous and ready to share, storing up for themselves the treasure of a good foundation for the future, so that they may take hold of that which is life indeed. 1 Tim. 6:17–19

6. We Are to Be Generous in Our Giving.

As we are intentionally generous with our finances for God's kingdom, we will see the message of Jesus continue to increase throughout the world, those in need cared for, and our hearts less controlled by money.

In the Old Testament, people were required by law to bring to the temple 10 to 23 per cent of their income. In the New Testament, generosity is determined to be a matter of the heart. We're to be guided by God's Spirit in us, our capacity, and the need to share in the expenses of the church we attend. We're called to equal sacrifice and a generosity that remembers that God's blessing outpaces our giving. The New Testament shares with us example of many believers who gave more than Old Testament tithing requirements. (Luke 6:38; Acts 4:34–37; 1 Cor. 16:2; 2 Cor. 8:11–15).

DISCUSSION

Why do we ignore talking about money as Christians?

_____

_____

_____

In what area do you need to work: finding employment, saving, investing, spending, or giving?

_____

_____

_____

Personal Application

_____

_____

_____

_____

_____

_____

_____

CHAPTER NOTES:

_____

_____

_____

_____

_____

_____

_____

_____

_____

_____

_____

_____

_____

_____

_____

_____

_____

_____

See Appendix for Q&A

OTHERS

"Love your neighbour as yourself." **Matt. 22:39**

CHAPTER 14

RELATIONSHIPS

We are created to walk in healthy relationships with each other. While that may not have been modelled to us, we have the opportunity and capacity to experience it in our own lives as we embrace biblical relationship principles.

READING

Eph. 5:1–6:9

THOUGHTS

Our ultimate goal is to walk in love in all our relationships. God continues to work on this in us and helps us understand what this looks like. Love is the perfect balance between grace and truth, freedom and boundaries. As we grow in our understanding of love, we will grow in healthy relationships (1 Cor. 13).

Not all relationships are created equal. We cannot give the same amount of time and focus to each connection. Setting relationship priorities helps us establish boundaries to protect ourselves and others around us. Here is a biblical view of priorities in relationships.

- God—Our relationship with God always comes first in our relationships. Our relationship with God is different than serving in the church.

- Marriage—If you're married, your marriage is your primary relationship.

- Children—If you have kids, they are your second priority.

- Parents—If your parents are alive, they are your third priority.

- Friendships—It's up to you to decide the order of importance of the friendships you have outside of these priorities. You can have an inner circle of close friends and concentric outer circles of acquaintances around you. Your friendships may or may not include extended family.

Marriage

We are designed to experience healthy, exclusive, lifelong marriage relationships. This partnership is intended for friendship, shared purpose, and procreation. God designed men to lay down their life in service to their wives willingly, and God created women to lay down their life in service to their husbands willingly as well. This ideal only works in a co-voluntary, non-demanded, serve-first approach (Eph. 5:3, 15–33).

Wives, submit to your husbands, as is fitting for those who belong to the Lord. Husbands, love your wives and never treat them harshly. Col. 3:18–19

Friendships

We can have good friendships by being friendly, discerning, and intentional, and by establishing boundaries and building trust over time (Prov. 13:20, 17:17, 18:24; John 15:13).

Two people are better off than one, for they can help each other succeed. If one person falls, the other can reach out and help. But someone who falls alone is in real trouble. Eccles. 4:9–10

Sexuality

We are created for monogamous sexual experiences in the context of heterosexual marriage. We will experience brokenness in activities outside of this. How does this view challenge your beliefs about sexuality (Rom. 1:26–27; 1 Cor. 6:9–18; Eph. 5:31, Heb. 13:4)?

The wife gives authority over her body to her husband, and the husband gives authority over his body to his wife. 1 Cor. 7:4

Parents

The primary role of parents is to nurture and train children to become healthy, self-sustaining adults who walk in relationship with God and fulfill their potential to join God in His mission (Deut. 6:6–9; Ps. 127:3–5; Prov. 29:17; Eph. 6:4; Col. 3:21; 2 Tim. 3:14–15).

Direct your children onto the right path, and when they are older, they will not leave it. Prov. 22:6

Children

The primary role of children is to obey their parents as they are nurtured to become healthy, self-sustaining adults fully devoted to Jesus (Prov. 1:8–9; Eph. 6:1–3).

Children, obey your parents because you belong to the Lord, for this is the right thing to do. Eph. 6:1

Employees & Employers

We are called to be diligent employees who give our best, or employers who serve, pay, and treat employees well (Eph. 6:5–9; Col. 4:1).

A New Way

We live in a world that challenges a biblical view of healthy relationships and sexuality. The biblical model might even contradict what you've personally believed up to this point and what you've experienced. You may have also encountered pain from past relationships. The good news is that no matter your past, you can write a new future.

DISCUSSION

How does the biblical model challenge you personally?

Why is God specific about our sexuality in the Bible?

List some of your questions related to relationships that you would like to further explore with a mentor.

Personal Application

CHAPTER NOTES:

See Appendix for Q&A

CHAPTER 15

CHURCH

You are connected to other followers of Jesus.

1 Cor. 12:12–27

When you come to faith, you become a child of God. As God's child, you become part of a worldwide spiritual family called the Church. The Church is not a building, a brand, or an institution. It's a group of imperfect people committed to Jesus, relationship with each other, and following in the way of Jesus together. The local church is a smaller expression of the worldwide Church, all connected because of a relationship with Jesus (1 Cor. 12:12–27; Eph. 2:19–22; 1 Pet. 2:5).

Get Connected

You are designed to get connected to a local church and not simply loosely affiliate with a particular building, attend a service when it's convenient, or watch an online experience. Getting connected to others gives you the opportunity to love unconditionally, live authentically, give and receive grace, walk in commitment and faithfulness, embrace different perspectives and preferences, and so much more (Matt. 18:20; John 13:35; Rom. 12:10–16; 1 Thess. 5:11; Heb. 10:24–25).

Be devoted to one another. Rom. 12:10

Characteristics of a Healthy Church

There's no perfect local group of followers of Jesus; however, there are some indications of a local church trending in an appropriate direction.

Healthy Churches

- They focus on Jesus's vision of making disciples and loving each other (Matt. 22:36–40, 28:19–20).

- They clearly teach and seek to be guided by the entire Bible (1 Cor. 15:1–8; Gal. 1:8; Phil. 2:1–10; Col. 2:18).

- They are organized and orderly with accountable leadership at every level (Acts 2:40–47, 6:3–4; 1 Cor. 14:26–33, 38–40; 1 Tim. 3; Titus 1:5; Rev. 1–3).

- They handle money with integrity (Luke 16:11; Titus 1:7), incur average operating expenses (1 Cor. 16:1–3), pay leaders a fair salary (Gal. 6:6, 1 Tim. 5:17–18), give a hand up to the genuinely needy in the church (Acts 4:35; 1 Tim. 5:9; James 2:15–16), and fund missions (Rom. 5:26; 2 Cor. 11:9).

Becoming a Local Church Member

It's essential to commit to the people of the church when you find a local church to be a part of. As you grow in your faith, you'll discover yourself moving from a life that's self-serving to a life that serves others. You'll see the church as a community to which to contribute more than an event to attend. Not only will you grow to love people, but you'll grow to share your time, talent, and treasure (Eph. 4).

DISCUSSION

Why are we tempted to look for a church to "get from" rather than "give to"?

Personal Application

CHAPTER NOTES:

See Appendix for Q&A

CHAPTER 16

YOUR STORY

We are designed to share our faith stories with others.

1 Pet. 3:15–16

The decision you made to follow Jesus and the changes you see in your life are not to be kept secret. It's good news that others need to know (John 1:35–51).

> Andrew, Simon Peter's brother, was one of these men who heard what John said and then followed Jesus. Andrew went to find his brother, Simon, and told him, "We have found the promised one from God ..." John 1:40–41

Are there people in your circle of influence you can invite to follow Jesus? Start by making a list of people you can pray for, share your story with, and invest in for the next year.

As you share your story with family, friends, neighbours, and coworkers, you'll help them understand the change that's happening in your life. You don't have to try to convince them. Simply share your story. No one has a story like yours.

I pray that you would be active in sharing your faith so that you might understand all the good things we have in Jesus. Philem. 1:6

Words

Share who you were before Jesus, how you came to follow Jesus, and what Jesus has done for you. Be authentic, as life isn't perfect. Be transparent about your struggles. Be real about the strength that God gives you each day. Sometimes preparing this ahead of time will prepare you for moments that come up. Write out your story in three easy points.

Life before Jesus:

How you came to faith:

What has changed in your life:

Prayer

As you ask God each day for opportunities to share your faith, He will bring them to you. You can also pray for boldness and courage over any fear (Acts 4:23–31).

Pray for us, too, that God will give us many opportunities to speak about Jesus. Col. 4:3.

Actions

Part of sharing your faith is living your faith. As your words, character, and habits change, people will begin to ask questions. What areas of your life take away from your story? These areas can be the ones you start to pray about, asking God to help you change and take steps to do something.

... let your good deeds shine out for all to see so that every- one will praise your heavenly Father. Matt. 5:16

Rejection

Not everyone will like the faith that you've chosen. As you are open about your new life, some of your friendships and relation- ships may be affected. You may be rejected and feel all alone. Therefore, it's important to belong to a community of faith who, like you, also have friends who may have dismissed them (Matt. 5:10–12; John 15:18–25).

Big Picture

As you share your faith, you join God in His mission of chang- ing the world one invitation at a time. As individuals follow Jesus, they begin the journey of experiencing who they were created to be. As we do this, the world becomes a better place (2 Cor. 5:11–21; Eph. 1).

DISCUSSION

Who are the people in your life who don't know your story?

_____

_____

_____

Do you struggle with fear in sharing your story?

_____

_____

_____

Personal Application

_____

_____

_____

_____

_____

_____

_____

_____

_____

_____

_____

_____

_____

_____

CHAPTER NOTES:

See Appendix for Q&A

CHAPTER 17

DISCIPLE-MAKING

BIG IDEA

You are a disciple-maker.

READING

Matt. 28:16–20

THOUGHTS

Jesus gave His first followers this final priority: to make disciples. To invest in people in the same way that He invested in them. Sharing our lives with others teaches them what we know and models what we are becoming. That same priority is the call of every follower of Jesus today. We're all called to invest in others around us by teaching and modelling the way of Jesus (John 1:38; 1 Cor. 4:17, 11:1).

Go and make disciples of all the nations, baptizing them in the name of the Father and the Son and the Holy Spirit. Teach these new disciples to obey all the commands I have given you. And be sure of this: I am with you always, even to the end of the age. Matt. 28:19–20

People

God places a small group of people in our lives for us to authentically and intentionally build relationships with and invest in. Sometimes that group of people can be informal, and sometimes it consists of leading a small group or class for kids or adults in your church.

Investing in others is one of the most rewarding activities we can get involved in. It can also be very difficult. It can be interruptive, disappointing, and time-consuming. Even Jesus had a follower who betrayed him. Yet as we invest in others, we find the blessing of spiritual growth.

The goal should be that after one to three years, these people can also invest in others so that the cycle can repeat itself (Matt. 4:18–21, 10:1-42; Luke 9–10; John 15:9–17).

Teach & Model

As you model your faith and teach what you know, you'll find that those you disciple will become who you are.

You have heard me teach things that have been confirmed by many reliable witnesses. Now teach these truths to other trustworthy people who will be able to pass them on to others. 2 Tim. 2:2

The focus of everything we teach always connects back to one of three areas: how to love God, ourselves, or others. While not exhaustive, here are some topics you can help people understand.

- God: How to pray and connect with God and study the Bible, the character and nature of God, the plan of God, and walking in the Spirit.

- Self: How you are created, healing, developing new thought patterns, forgiveness, discovering your gifts, how to manage money and resources.

- Others: friendships, marriage, parenthood, serving in mission, sharing your faith

Make a list of other topics that interest you that aren't mentioned above. As you invest your life in someone else, you can teach that topic too.

There are many ways to intentionally invest in the person you're discipling. Some people make a list of Bible verses and discuss them from week to week. Others pick a book like this one to help foster discussion along the way. No matter your method, the key is to start. As you do, you will join God in His mission that the whole world will hear the message of Jesus and daily grow in becoming who He has designed them to be.

Make a shortlist of three people who you know that are newer to the faith. Decide to start a group and invite them to join you for the next year.

DISCUSSION

How can intentionally investing in others be interruptive to normal life?

Who has been instrumental in your journey of faith and shared their life with you?

Personal Application

CHAPTER NOTES:

See Appendix for Q&A

THEOLOGY

The Bible, Creeds, God, Realms, Angels &
Demons, Humanity, Sin, Salvation

CHAPTER 18

THE BIBLE

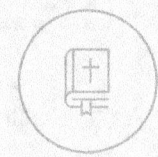

Learning to value and understanding how to apply the Bible are essential parts of being a follower of Jesus.

2 Tim. 3:16; 2 Pet. 1:20–21

Opening the Bible

If you open the Bible to the first few pages, you'll find a table of contents. You'll see two parts: the Hebrew scriptures (Old Testament) and Christian writings (New Testament). Of the sixty-six books, thirty-nine are in the Old Testament and twenty-seven in the New.

The Bible was first written in Hebrew, Aramaic, and Koine Greek. We have a variety of English versions because translators took a different approach in each.

There are literal "word for word" translations such as the NKJV, NASB, RSV, and ESV. There are dynamic equivalent translations that translate the text thought for thought, such as the NIV, NEV, and NLT. Some versions are more the personal interpretations of the translators, called paraphrases, such as The Message and the Living Bible.How Did We Get the Bible?

Old Testament

The first part of the Bible is composed of the Hebrew writings. They're included in scripture based entirely on the Jewish community's acceptance of them as authentic and their careful transmission over the centuries.

The Hebrew writings were initially written in Hebrew and Aramaic by forty authors over a thousand years on wood, stone, clay, papyrus, and parchment. Scribes meticulously and accurately hand-copied these early texts. Today, there are thousands of copies available in different languages from various locations and eras. While there are minor transmission errors, overall the Old Testament demonstrates a high level of preservation consistency.

Historians suggest that the Old Testament was assimilated and compiled during four significant periods: after the exodus, at the introduction of kings, during the fall of Jerusalem, and when those exiled returned to Jerusalem under Ezra and Nehemiah. During each of these periods, leaders applied an early test to determine if God inspired the writing.

In Deuteronomy 18:22, the test is outlined. If a person's predictions came true, and there was an external supernatural sign that the community recognized, then the words were considered divine. If prophets failed, then people should realize that the person was not speaking for God. Also, all the authors of the books held the divinely appointed office of judge, prophet, priest, or king.

The New Testament

Within twenty years of Jesus's life, several dozen books and teachings about Him began to appear. There were also many contradictory reports of His teachings that began to circulate.

Jesus's inner circle (called Apostles) and their apprentices began to record what He had done and said. Jesus had commissioned them to do so and promised to divinely speak through them (Matt. 10:11–20, 28:18). Even though some of the Apostles were professionally trained in tachygraphy and could easily transcribe all Jesus said exactly, there was a feeling that God was supernaturally guiding all they were writing (John in Rev. 1:1–3; Peter in 2 Pet. 3:15–16; Paul in Acts 9, 1 Cor. 14:37–38, Gal. 2, 1 Thess. 2:13).

In addition to the Hebrew writings, the Apostles' writings were also copied and circulated in local churches. Each week they would read passages from both the Old and New Testament in their gatherings (Col. 4:16; 1 Thess. 5:27; 1 Tim. 4:13; Rev. 1:3). The early copies came in a codex format for reading rather than Greco Roman artistic form. Early church fathers such as Ignatius (30–107 AD), Clement (30–100 AD), Polycarp (65–155 AD), Papias (70–155 AD), Irenaeus, (120–202 AD), and Justin Martyr (110–165 AD) all quoted from the entire collection. The council of Nicaea (325 AD) and the council of Constantinople (381 AD) later affirmed this early tradition.

Together

While the Bible existed in Koine Greek, the entire Old and New Testament were first combined and translated into another language (Latin) around 400 AD by St. Jerome. Other similar translations emerged as well.

John Wycliffe completed the first English translation of the Bible in the late fourteenth century. Scribes were commissioned to make copies until the advancement of the printing press in Europe in 1460, when entire copies of the Bible were available for everyone.

New translations depended on the availability of much older

Hebrew and Greek copies. Today we have over 5,500 complete or fragmented Greek manuscripts, 9,000 Latin manuscripts and 9,000 manuscripts in Armenian, Coptic, Ethiopian, Slavic, and Syriac.

What about My Questions?

The way you see the Bible will determine how you approach it. If you see it as myth, then you'll approach it as a collection of fairy tales. If you see it as a book of great ideas, then you will approach it as self-help advice. If you see it as a story, you'll approach it as narrative history.

Many people have concerns with the Bible. Some point out textual contradictions between different verses, whether it's simple facts like Jehoiachin and Ahaziah's age when they became king, the number of stalls Solomon had for horses, the number of animals in the ark, or differing genealogical records.

Some wonder how much is literal and how much is symbolic. Was the entire world created in seven days, or through a process over millions of years? Did the worldwide flood happen, or was it only local? Was there an exodus out of Egypt through the Red Sea? Do miracles happen, or is there a way to easily explain them away?

Some have a challenge reconciling modern values with ancient directives. How do we understand Old Testament law? How do we deal with ancient slavery and the treatment of women? How do we consider gender identity and sexuality? How do we approach capitalism, socialism, nationalism, globalism, pacifism, gun control, environmentalism?

Some have a problem reconciling the life and message of Jesus with how the Old Testament portrays God. How do we approach a book representing a loving God in one section and a God who gets violent in other spaces? Is God any different than ancient pagan gods and goddesses? What part does God play in natural disasters?

I would suggest that rather than embracing these questions as unanswerable, you begin a journey through the Bible's pages, open to the possibility that the answers will emerge over time and that there is a reality behind the words you apply to your life.

I have learned as a finite human being living with other finite human beings that questions are simply an indication that there is much to learn. The answers are there. One needs to keep asking questions until a solution is found.

How Do I Approach the Bible?

For thousands of years, people have been asking questions about life, yet no matter how many experiences we've had, we're all limited by space and time. No one has an advantage—no one past and no one present.

Most belief systems in the world rest on humans who claim to have figured out life. The big claim of Jesus is that He is the creator of all that we see. He claimed to be outside the universe, becoming human to help give us an outside perspective and live life as He designed it to be.

Jesus fulfilled hundreds of predictions by Jewish prophets who spoke over several hundred years. These prophets claimed that God was speaking to them. When Jesus fulfilled their prophecies, He validated their claims. Some have observed that the Old Testament has 456 predictions of Jesus with 558 supporting fulfillments (see Appendix).

Yet more than this, Jesus validated other things they had written. Over sixty recorded times, Jesus validated the Old Testament as historically accurate and divine in authorship (Matt. 4:4, 5:17–18, 15:3, 22:31; Luke 24:25–53; John 17:17). Here are a few of the things that Jesus confirms.

Moses as the author of the first five books of the Bible, and all that he wrote as true and not primarily mythical or symbolic (Matt. 5:17, 8:4; John 5:45–47).

Hard-to-believe stories like creation (Matt. 19:4–5), the world-wide flood (Matt. 24:37–39), the destruction of Sodom (Matt. 10:15; Luke 17:32;), Israel's deliverance from Egypt and wandering in the wilderness (Matt. 12:3–4; John 6:31, 7:22), and Jonah and the whale (Matt. 12:39–41).

Key figures such as Abraham (John 8:56), Isaac and Jacob (Matt. 8:11), Moses (John 7:22), David (Matt. 12:3), Solomon (Matt. 6:29), Elijah (Matt. 17:11), Elisha (Luke 4:27), and Zechariah (Luke 11:51).

The authorship of other books and stories, such as Daniel (Matt. 24:15) and Isaiah (Matt. 8:17; Luke 4:17-19; John 12:38–41).

As a result, followers of Jesus see these writings as inspired by God. Jesus also encouraged His first followers to pass on His life and message to the world (Matt. 28:18-20; Rev. 1:11).

For Jesus's first followers, He was the point of scripture. Not only had He commissioned them to pass on His life and message, but He had also verified the Old Testament. Here are some of the ways they articulated their view of Scripture (Old Testament).

All Scripture is inspired by God and is useful to teach us what is true and to make us realize what is wrong in our lives. It corrects us when we are wrong and teaches us to do what is right. 2 Tim. 3:16

Above all, you must realize that no prophecy in Scripture ever came from the prophet's understanding or human initiative. No, those prophets were moved by the Holy Spirit, and they spoke from God 2 Pet. 1:20–21

This is how we got both the Jewish writings (Old Testament) and the Christian writings (New Testament). We can see that the Bible isn't merely a book of things that people have said but a collection of the things that God has said through people.

The clear perspective they had was that the Bible is the very Word of God—not merely human in origin with divine influence but spoken by God through human beings. For the first followers of Jesus, God is the speaker; the Bible is His speech, and the people to whom He speaks are both past and present (Hebrews 1).

We believe the Bible is God's Word. It's our guide. It's where we get our information about God and life. It's how we know what is real and true. Rather than trusting ourselves as the source of what is true, we choose to put our faith in the God of the Bible, who speaks.

As you see the Bible as God's Word, you will have a source to find the answers to the questions you're asking. The Bible is not to be worshipped but read as a record of relationships with people. As you learn to read and interpret the Bible, it will change your life.

DISCUSSION

Why is the history of the transmission of the Bible so important?

What challenges do you have with the idea that the Bible is divinely inspired?

If the Bible is what it says it is, how does that change how I approach it?

Personal Application

CHAPTER NOTES:

See Appendix for Q&A

CHAPTER 19

CREEDS

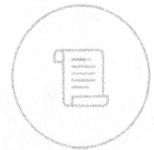

Creeds are imperfect summaries of what we believe.

In the early church, simple creeds were developed to summarize the main point of the Bible storyline. A person often recited these creeds before baptism to affirm their understanding and intention to follow Jesus. Here are two early ones.

> Christ was revealed in a human body and vindicated by the Spirit. He was seen by angels and announced to the nations. He was believed in throughout the world and taken to heaven in glory. 1 Tim. 3:16

> I passed on to you what was most important and what had also been passed on to me. Christ died for our sins, just as the Scriptures said. He was buried, and he was raised from the dead on the third day, just as the Scriptures said. 1 Cor. 15:3–4

Over time, these creeds grew to articulate other aspects of the main message. Some of the most popular creeds are the Apostles' Creed and the Nicene Creed.

The Apostles Creed

I believe in God, the Father almighty, creator of heaven and earth. I believe in Jesus Christ, God's only Son, our Lord, who was conceived by the Holy Spirit, born of the Virgin Mary, suffered under Pontius Pilate, was crucified, died, and was buried; He descended to the dead. On the third day, He rose again; He ascended into heaven, He is seated at the right hand of the Father, and He will come to judge the living and the dead. I believe in the Holy Spirit, the holy Catholic Church, the communion of saints, the forgiveness of sins, the resurrection of the body, and the life everlasting. Amen.

The Nicene Creed

We believe in one God, the Father, the Almighty, maker of heaven and earth, of all that is, seen and unseen. We believe in one Lord, Jesus Christ, the only Son of God, eternally begotten of the Father, God from God, Light from Light, true God from true God, begotten, not made, of one Being with the Father; through him, all things were made. For us and for our salvation, he came down from heaven, was incarnate of the Holy Spirit and the Virgin Mary and became truly human. For our sake, he was crucified under Pontius Pilate; he suffered death and was buried. On the third day, he rose again in accordance with the Scriptures; he ascended into heaven and is seated at the right hand of the Father. He will come again in glory to judge the living and the dead, and His Kingdom will have no end. We believe in the Holy Spirit, the Lord, the giver of life, who proceeds from the Father [and the Son], who with the Father and the Son is worshipped and glorified, who has spoken through the prophets. We believe in one holy catholic and apostolic Church. We acknowledge one baptism for the forgiveness of sins. We look for the resurrection of the dead and the life of the world to come. Amen.

While no creed is all-encompassing, we will attempt to understand some of the more essential concepts and themes discussed throughout the Bible. Creeds are a written summary of our convictions. As we articulate our beliefs, they affect our behaviour. It is good to review the creed or statement of faith of the church you attend.

DISCUSSION

How do you feel about creeds? What is helpful and potentially hurtful about them?

Personal Application

CHAPTER NOTES:

See Appendix for Q&A

CHAPTER 20

GOD

As we understand God's character and nature, we better understand life.

Exod. 33 & 34

What Is God Like?

There's something inside all of us that's aware of God but isn't sure what He's like and how He works. The good news is that even though God is incomprehensible (Job 11:7; John 1:18), He has revealed Himself to us (John 1:18). God has revealed Himself to humanity in many ways. We can see God in creation (Rom. 1:20), in Jesus (Heb. 1:1–3), and in the Bible (John 1).

As we grow in our relationship with God, we come to realize that He's not as simple and one dimensional as a pantheistic deity. God is multifaceted and complex. The Bible is the record of God's interaction with thousands of people over time. Those interactions give us a picture of God. Here are some specific characteristics we find.

- Creator of everything: God is the source and creator of everything (Gen. 1:1; Neh. 9:6; Ps. 115:15, 121:2; Col. 1:16–17; John 1:3; Rev. 4:11). Therefore, moving away from Him leads to levels of death. This is why we value life. This is why we look to Him for everything.

- Transcendent: God is not human. He's not like us. He is "other" (Acts 17:24–29). This is why we can't humanize Him and reduce Him to a human being.

- Self-existent/self-sustaining: God has not been created and He does not need anyone to sustain Him (John 5:26). This is why we elevate our view of who He is.

- All-powerful (omnipotent): There is nothing that has more power than God (Jer. 32:17). This means that God will do what He wants to do and doesn't need our permission to do it.

- Always present (omnipresent): The Bible tells us that because we exist within a realm of God, He is everywhere all the time. There is nowhere we can go where God isn't aware (Ps. 139; Jer. 23:23–24).

- All-knowing (omniscient): God is the focal point and source of all wisdom and understanding. He knows all. He sees the beginning from the end (Isa. 40:13–14).

- Unchanging (immutable): God does not change. He stays the same. He's always been the same. He hasn't evolved. He does not need to "grow up" (Mal. 3:6; James 1:17).

The Essence of God

God has eternally existed as a unified three-person entity, as Father, Son, and Spirit, who are equally God (character, attributes, what is true about Him), and individual yet "one." They each have different functions and roles. The word used to describe this reality is "Trinity."

Often, it's difficult to picture it. How can three separate entities be the same entity? No matter how hard we try to describe what God is like, our metaphors fall short. In the Trinity there is a mystery of God that we can appreciate but have a hard time articulating and fully understanding. As we search the Scripture, we grow to see and discover this complex arrangement.

The name of God, "Elohim," occurs over 2,250 times in the Bible. This word is plural in nature and signifies three persons (Genesis 1:26; Isaiah 6:8). Yet other scriptures also talk about God as completely unified and singular in nature (Deut. 6:4; 1 Cor. 8:6). This is how we get the idea of three persons in one (Matt. 3:16–17; Mark 1:9–11; Luke 3:21–22; John 1:32–34; Rom. 15:30; 1 Cor. 12:5–7, 13:14; Gal. 4:6; Eph. 4:4–6, 5:18–20; 2 Thess. 2:13–14; 1 Pet. 1:2).

What Motivates God?

Perfect love is the cornerstone of God's character and nature. While our finite mind may take an eternity to grasp an infinite God and His love fully, we can get a glimpse of it from scripture. "God is love" (Rom. 8:37–39; Eph. 3:14–21; 1 John 4:8, 5:7, 14:7–18, 21:25). God's love is seen in His:

- Goodness: God's goodness speaks of the nature of His love. God operates with the best long-term intentions in mind (Ps. 73:1; Rom. 8:28).

- Faithfulness: God's faithfulness speaks of the constancy of His love. God doesn't stop operating with a heart of love (Deut. 7:9).

- Justice: God's justice speaks of the equal distribution of His love. God will set everything right with everyone and in every case. God will allow everyone to experience the ends of their own decisions and ensure that His scales of justice have been satisfied for each person who is affected by the decisions of others (Exod. 34:6–7; Ps. 19:7–11).

- Holiness (righteous, true): God's holiness speaks of the quantity and purity of His love. He is full of love, all the time. His actions are entirely pure in their motivation and practice (Matt. 22:36–40; Eph. 1:4).

- Mercy & Grace: God's mercy and grace speak of the extensiveness of His love. God gives second chances and provides ways and means of forgiveness (Eph. 2:4–9).

- Sovereignty: God's sovereignty speaks of the power and authority of His love. He can give reason to the chaos we create, using it to fulfill His ultimate purpose (Rom. 8:28, 38–39).

- Emotions: God's feelings—even what we'd consider negative emotions—reflect His love. God gets angry when anything begins to threaten His beautiful creation (Ps. 30:5). God's love causes Him deep pain (Isa. 53:3–8). He hates anything that promises what only He can offer us (Hos. 6:6; Matt. 12:7, 15:8; Luke 13:34; James 4:5).

God's love is seen in His names. Here are a few that we see in Scripture.

- JEHOVAH-ROHI—meaning "The Lord my shepherd" (Ps. 23:1)

- JEHOVAH-SHAMMAH—meaning "The Lord who is present" (Ezek. 48:35)

- JEHOVAH-RAPHA—meaning "The Lord our healer" (Exod. 15:26)

- JEHOVAH-TSIDKENU—meaning "The Lord our righteousness" (Jer. 23:6)

- JEHOVAH-JIREH—meaning "The Lord will provide" (Gen. 22:13–14)

- JEHOVAH-NISSI—meaning "The Lord's presence gives us victory" (Exod. 17:15)

- JEHOVAH-SHALOM—meaning "The Lord is peace" (Judg. 6:24)

- JEHOVAH-SABAOTH–meaning "The Lord of Hosts" (Isa. 6:1–3)

DISCUSSION

How does our understanding of God shape how we live?

_____

_____

_____

How does each of God's attributes change the way we approach life?

_____

_____

_____

How does the lens of love change the way we see the attributes of God?

_____

_____

_____

Personal Application

_____

_____

_____

_____

_____

_____

_____

CHAPTER NOTES:

See Appendix for Q&A

CHAPTER 21

REALMS

BIG IDEA

As we know where everything happens, it will help us understand our place in this world.

READING

2 Cor. 4

THOUGHTS

Depending on how you were raised, you may have different ideas about the existence of a reality other than the natural world. There are different views of the spiritual world.

- Naturalistic: Since the seventeenth century, when empiricism and rationalism gave birth to naturalism, there's been a view that what we see is all there is. Concepts such as angels, demons, and the Holy Spirit are viewed as pure myth and a product of our imagination.

- The Superstitious: For much of human history, people have believed that there is a reality beyond what we see. However, these believers vary in their opinion about how we ought to interact with this reality. In this view, there are spirits, but we must figure out how to harness or avoid their power.

So Where Does Everything Happen?

While physicists have different explanations of how many different dimensions exist, the Bible clearly outlines four different realities that we can be sure of: the physical world, the spiritual world, eternal heaven, and the separated realm of hell.

Physical World

This is the world where we live, can see, and interact with. This includes our entire seen universe. This is the world we are most aware of. This is the world we are born into and the world we leave (Gen. 1:1).

Spiritual World

This is the unseen world between eternal heaven and the physical world. This is where demons and angels interact (Gen. 28:12; 2 Kings 6; Ezek. 8:3; Eph. 6:12). It's most often referred to as "between heaven and earth," or "heavenlies/heavenly places." What we do on earth affects this world. What happens in this world affects the physical realm.

Eternal Heaven

This is the place where God resides eternally (2 Cor. 4:18, 5:1). It's the realm that rules (Josh. 2:11; Ps. 102:19, 135:6; Dan. 4:26, 35; Matt. 6:10, 16:19). It's referenced in the Bible as the "third heaven" (2 Cor. 12:2) and the "heaven of heavens" (Deut. 10:14; Neh. 9:6). Hebrews 8–10 (particularly 8:1–5, 9:1–5, 24–25) illustrates this in more detail.

Hell

This is a real place prepared for demons and those who reject

God's rule of their life. This place is completely separated from other creatures. This is not a symbolic place (Matt. 13:49–50, 25:31–46; 2 Thess. 1:8–10; Rev. 20:10–18; 21:7–8).

DISCUSSION

What hints for the existence of the unseen world and the eternal world are there around us?

_____

_____

_____

How does the idea of hell/heaven go against science and our culture?

_____

_____

_____

List other questions you would like to discuss with your mentor

_____

_____

_____

Personal Application

_____

_____

_____

_____

_____

CHAPTER NOTES:

_____

_____

_____

_____

_____

_____

_____

_____

_____

_____

_____

_____

_____

_____

_____

_____

See Appendix for Q&A

CHAPTER 22

ANGELS & DEMONS

God created spiritual beings called angels and demons.

Heb. 1

Angels are not dead relatives or mystical spirits, nor are they the personification of our positive or negative emotions. Angels are special beings created by God with celestial/heavenly bodies (Ps. 148:2,5; Col. 1:16; Heb. 11:14; Rev. 4:11, 5:13).

Angels are intelligent (Matt. 8:29; 2 Cor. 11:3; 1 Pet. 1:12), show emotion (Luke 2:13; James 2:19; Rev. 12:17), and exercise their own will (Luke 8:28-31; 2 Tim.. 2:26; Jude 6). Angels were created by God to declare and promote the glory and will of God.

- A. Physical Realm: Angels actively execute God's desires in our world. Angels are God's agents to bring about God's ultimate will in our society—whatever it may be at a particular point in time (Gen. 28:12; Ps. 103:20; Matt. 13:41, 24:31; Luke 2:15; Heb. 1:7, 2:2; Rev. 7:1; 8:2). Today, angels are sent by God to help believers (Heb. 1:14). They observe Christian life and suffering (1 Cor. 4:9, 11:10; Eph. 3:10; 1 Pet. 1:12). They encourage and comfort (Acts 27:23–24) and care for the righteous at death (Luke 16:22). They reveal God's response to prayer (Acts 12:5–10). They help win those far from God (Acts 8:26, 10:3).

- B. Spiritual Realm: In the spiritual realm, God's angels battle fallen angels, called demons (Rev. 12:7–9; Daniel 10), on their way to exercise God's will in the earth.

- C. In Eternal Heaven: Angels eternally worship and give glory to God (Ps. 103:20, 148:1–2; Isa. 6:1–3; Heb. 1:6; Rev. 4–5, 22:9).

God created angels in a hierarchy of authority. This same hierarchy is continued to this day. (Col. 1:15–16; 1 Pet. 3:22). While angels are mentioned over two hundred times in the Bible, and there is different speculation about them, we do know the following types of angels exist: Seraphim (Isa. 6:1–2), Cherubim (Exod. 25:20, 26:31; Ezek. 26:1; Heb. 9:50), and Archangels (Jude 1:9).

Who is Satan and What Are Demons?

Satan was a lead angel in heaven who oversaw over one-third of all the angels. He managed all the music in Heaven (Ezek. 28:13–14), but because he and the angels he oversaw rebelled against God, he was thrown out of heaven by God (Isa. 14:12–14; Rev. 12:7–9). He and his angels lost their heavenly bodies, and together they look for physical bodies to live in (Matt. 12:43–45; Luke 11:24). Satan and his demons (fallen angels) are not omnipresent, omnipotent, or omniscient, yet they are very highly organized (Col. 1:15–16).

In the beginning, Satan deceived Adam and Eve and gained authority in the earth (Gen. 1:26; 2 Cor. 4:4). But because of Jesus, he lost his influence in the earth (Eph. 1:16–23; 1 John 3:8). Today, we are in the process of the restoration of God's authority in the earth. Today, Satan Is powerless against Christ's followers (Eph. 2:4–6) and has an eternity prepared for Him in the separation realm of hell (Matt. 25:41).

Demons are under Satan's strict orders and accredited with a variety of different types of activities:

- stealing, killing, and destroying God's good creation (John 10:10)

- accusing believers before God (Rev. 12:10)

- deceiving and tempting (John 8:44; 1 Pet. 5:8; Rev. 12:9)

- causing false visions and dreams (Jer. 14:14; Zech. 10:2; Matt. 4)

- making evil appear harmless (2 Cor. 11:14)

- lying (1 Kings 22:19–22)

- creating fear (Rom. 8:15; 2 Tim. 1:7)

- tempting (Matt. 4:1–11; 1 John 2:15–17)

- dividing people (Judg. 9:22–24)

- causing tormenting thoughts (1 Sam. 16:14–16,23)

- bringing the affliction of some sicknesses – (Job; Matt. 9:32–33, 12:22)

- channeling (1 Chron. 10:13; Isa. 8:19)

DISCUSSION

How does our culture view angels and demons?

How do angels interact with Christians?

Why do Satan and demons strike fear into people?

Personal Application

CHAPTER NOTES:

See Appendix for Q&A

CHAPTER 23

HUMANITY

As we understand how we are created, we will understand ourselves better.

Ps. 139

God creates us in three distinct but interwoven parts: body, soul, and spirit (Gen. 1:26–27, 2:7; Job 7:11; Heb. 4:12).

Now may the God of peace Himself sanctify you entirely; and may your spirit and soul and body be preserved complete, without blame at the coming of our Lord Jesus Christ. 1 Thess. 5:23

Body

The body is the part of us that helps us connect with our environment and others around us in the natural world. It's made up of our physical senses (taste, touch, sight, hearing, smell). It receives information from our physical environment and manifests what our soul decides to do with that information in particular (Gen. 2:7, 18:27; Job 34:15; Ps. 90:3; Isa. 64:8).

Soul

The soul is made up of our mind, heart, and emotions. It influences our body and is connected to the spirit. The mind receives and analyzes what comes from the physical world. It stores memories of past experiences and perceptions. It influences the body's actions. Its conclusions and preferred activities are based on the focus of the heart.

The heart is the centre of intention in our being. It influences all we do. Its motives are formed by the voice it listens to and trusts in outside of itself. Both the mind and the spirit control it. Its primary function is to decide what voice to hear. It is "the will" of who we are. It can be focused on the natural world (as understood in the mind and received through the senses, whether from God or another voice), or can focus on the Spirit of God.

The emotions are the product of fulfilled/unfulfilled expectations based on belief founded in experiential (what we have experienced) and empirical (what we think ought to be) understanding. Emotions are a result of the interaction of the heart and the mind (Num. 16:22, 27:16; Ps. 139:14; Eccles. 12:7; Isa. 42:5; Zech. 12:1; 1 Cor. 15:45).

Spirit

The part of us that holds God's Spirit. Through this connection, God's nature can affect our soul and body (Num. 16:22, 27:16; Eccles. 12:7; Isa. 42:5; Zech. 12:1).

Interactions

All of me interacts with all of me. One part affects the other: spirit/body (1 Kings 21:5; James 2:26), soul/spirit (Deut. 2:30; Job 7:11; Ps. 51:10, 51:17, 77:6, 78:8, 143:4; Prov. 15:13, 17:22; Isa. 57:15,

65:14; Lam. 1:20), body/soul/spirit (Exod. 35:21; Prov. 15:13; Lam. 2:11; Ezek. 21:7; Dan. 5:20).

Purpose

Why are we here? What is our purpose? This is a major theme that we can see through the entire Bible. It gets started right at the beginning.

Then God said, "Let us make human beings in our image, to be like us. They will reign over the fish in the sea, the birds in the sky, the livestock, all the wild animals on the earth, and the small animals that scurry along the ground." So God created human beings in his image. In the image of God, he created them; male and female, he created them. Then God blessed them and said, "Be fruitful and multiply. Fill the earth and govern it. Reign over the fish in the sea, the birds in the sky, and all the animals that scurry along the ground." Gen. 1:26–28 (emphasis added)

In the beginning, we see that God creates everything good. He creates humanity (male and female) in His image and gives them the power and ability to multiply themselves and govern creation.

The phrase "in God's image" appears many times throughout the Bible and explains our purpose. The idea is that as a mirror, shadow, or odour is merely a reflection of a source, so we as human beings are a reflection in the earth of who God is over everything. We are not God, but we mirror Him. Theologians sometimes summarize this by stating that humanity is created for "the glory of God" or "to worship God" (Gen. 1:26–27, 2:7, 5:1, 6:6, 9:6; Deut. 4:32; Ps. 39:5, 89:47, 104:30; Eccles. 11:5; Isa. 43:7, 45:12; Mal. 2:10; Matt. 19:4; John 1:3; Acts 17:26; Col. 1:16; Rev. 4:11).

DISCUSSION

Explain the spirit, soul, and body and how they interact together. If it's helpful, draw a diagram of this reality.

Describe the difference between knowing something in your mind and sensing something in your spirit.

Personal Application

CHAPTER NOTES:

_____

_____

_____

_____

_____

_____

_____

_____

_____

_____

_____

_____

_____

_____

_____

See Appendix for Q&A

CHAPTER 24

SIN

BIG IDEA

We do not have to let sin destroy us.

READING

Rom. 1

THOUGHTS

Limitations

God doesn't leave creation alone. In the beginning, He is actively involved in planting, hydrating, and growing the garden. He interacts very personally with humanity and places them in the garden to care for it. He encourages humanity to eat the fruit of every tree except the tree of the knowledge of good and evil. He warns humanity that death awaits those who consume its fruit.

The Lord God placed the man in the Garden of Eden to tend and watch over it. But the Lord God warned him, "You may freely eat the fruit of every tree in the garden— except the tree of the knowledge of good and evil. If you eat its fruit, you are sure to die." Gen. 2:15–17

Temptation

Satan (Isa. 14:12–13; Matt. 12:43; Luke 10:18, 11:24) seduces humanity to question the limitations God places on them. Satan questions the validity and the weight of the prohibition. He asks about God's motivations, intentionality, and the literal meaning of the boundary. He challenges the result of disobedience. He invites humanity into the place of God rather than dependency on Him.

> "You won't die!" the serpent replied to the woman. "God knows that your eyes will be opened as soon as you eat it, and you will be like God, knowing both good and evil." Gen. 3:4–5

Sin Enters

Satan convinces humanity to take of the tree. Humanity uses its criterion to determine that the tree and fruit seem good to eat. Humanity wants to be like God—to have the wisdom and experience not only of good but also evil. Humanity wants independence from the limitations of God and decides to disobey God and trust Satan's voice and their inner voice. Sin enters at this moment. Because God is love, He allows humanity to make choices and experience the outcome of their decisions.

> The woman was convinced. She saw that the tree was beautiful, and its fruit looked delicious, and she wanted the wisdom it would give her. So she took some of the fruit and ate it. Then she gave some to her husband, who was with her, and he ate it, too. Gen. 3:6

Immediate Consequences

Immediately, humanity loses the innocence that comes from dependency, experiences shame, tries to cover their guilt, and hides from God. God searches for humanity and outlines the results of their choice to be self-sufficient.

- On Satan: God curses Satan's earthly existence and foretells the hostility between humanity and Satan. We see that Satan will influence humanity but will ultimately be destroyed by one of Eve's descendants.

And I will cause hostility between you and the woman, and between your offspring and her offspring. He will strike your head, and you will strike his heel." (Gen. 3:15)

- On Humanity: Humanity is removed from the garden to experience independence. The woman will experience pain in child birth and the desire but inability to control her husband. The man will experience a cursed earth, causing a lifetime of struggle and work.

At that moment, their eyes were opened, and they suddenly felt shame ... So they hid from the Lord ... Then he said to the woman, "I will sharpen the pain of your pregnancy...and you will desire to control your husband, but he will rule over you"... And to the man, the ground is cursed because of you... all your life, and you will struggle...by the sweat of your brow"... So the Lord God banished them from the Garden of Eden, and he sent Adam out to cultivate the ground from which he had been made. Gen. 3:7–24

Long-Term Results

There are long term effects to sin.

- A) A sinful nature is passed on to every human being. This propensity to reject God is ingrained in us from birth. Each of us has sinned since being born. Each of us is a "slave" to sin and has come under its power (Gen. 8:21; Ps. 14:1–3; Isa. 53:6; Rom. 3:10, 23, 5:12, 6:16–22).

- B) Sin is the path to death. When we separate ourselves from God (source of life) and the parameters He has established, we experience varying degrees of death in our mind, bodies, relationships, and the world (Prov. 10:16;

Rom. 6:23, 7:5). We experience physical death, which is the passing from this world (Gen. 6:3). We also experience eternal death (Matt. 10:28, 18:8; Rev. 21:8).

What Does Sin Look Like?

As we have learned, sin is an attitude that begins with the desire to live independently from God, who is the source of life and love. Throughout the Bible, God reveals lists of actions that reflect this attitude.

The Conscience and The Voice: In the Old Testament, up to Moses's arrival, we see that the entry of sin consciousness in every individual (Gen. 3:22). The awareness of good and evil is built into every human being from this point on. We also see at the beginning the personal nature of the relationship God has with people: Adam and Eve (Gen. 3:8), Enoch (Gen. 5:22–24), Abraham (Gen. 17:1), Isaac (Gen. 26:24), Jacob (Gen. 35:9), and Noah (Gen. 6:13). God would speak, and people would listen. Sin was disobedience to God's voice.

The Law: After rescuing Israel from slavery in Egypt, God gives the nation of Israel a Top 2 and a Top 10: The Shema (Deut. 6:5) and the Ten Commandments (Exod. 20) summarize what it means to live right. God then speaks through Moses and gives regulations about temple worship, nation-building, social structure, health and dietary function, etc. In total, we find 613 laws designed to articulate what it looks like to promote life and the nation's advancement.

Jesus: Jesus emphasizes the Shema as the ultimate articulation of right and wrong—and what it means to listen to one's conscious.

Jesus replied, "'You must love the LORD your God with all your heart, all your soul, and all your mind.' This is the first and greatest commandment. A second is equally important: 'Love your neighbour as yourself.' The entire law and all the

demands of the prophets are based on these two command-
ments." Matt. 22:37-40

Jesus reinforces the Old Testament Law as having originated from God. He emphasizes the recognition of sin and a humane and compassionate approach to the sinner (John 8). Those who are not born Jewish are not required to keep the Law but the spirit and heart of the Law that Jesus emphasized (Acts 15; Rom. 6:12–14).

The Church

In the many letters to the first followers of Jesus, we see an emphasis of the idea that all of us have a conscience that directs us. We also know that we tend to ignore it, justify our actions, and lose sight of right and wrong (John 3:19; Rom. 2:15, 3:23, 14:1–23).

Lists of what it looks like to sin were also communicated as an outflow of this idea that sin is living independently from God and not living with love for Him and others (Rom. 1:26–32; Gal. 5:19–21; Eph. 5:3–7; 1 Tim. 1:9–10).

DISCUSSION

What activities did you not categorized as a sin in the past that you do now?

_____

_____

_____

Why do we like to ignore the idea of sin?

_____

_____

_____

Personal Application

_____

_____

_____

_____

_____

_____

_____

_____

_____

_____

_____

_____

_____

_____

CHAPTER NOTES:

_____
_____
_____
_____
_____
_____
_____
_____
_____
_____
_____
_____
_____
_____
_____
_____
_____

See Appendix for Q&A

CHAPTER 25

SALVATION

We are in the midst of being saved.

Rom. 8

The Plan

God provided a plan of salvation from sin and its effects from the moment it entered the world. The storyline of the Bible documents the revelation and outworking of this plan.

God reveals this plan to several people throughout history before it happens. Each of these encounters helps to uncover a different aspect of this plan.

Some of the more prominent encounters include Eve (Gen. 3:15), Abraham (Gen. 12:3), Jacob (Gen. 35:10–13), Samuel (2 Sam. 14:14), David (2 Sam. 7:1–16; Ps. 22), Isaiah (Isa. 9:6–7, 53), Jeremiah (Jer. 23:5, 33:15), Micah (Mic. 5:2), and Zechariah (Zech. 9:9).

The basic plan was to set up the nation of Israel, through whom He would come as a sinless baby (Isa. 9:6–7; Luke 2) to feel sin's effects and temptation (Isa. 53, Heb. 2:17–18, 4:15), to demonstrate God's power over sin in His life, to voluntarily die on the cross as a sacrifice for sin (Lev. 17:11; Is 53:3–10; John 10:17–18; 2 Cor. 5:21; Eph. 5:2; Heb. 9:22–26, 10:12; 1 Pet. 3:18; Rev. 5:6–10), to be raised from the dead with power over death (Rom. 8:34–35; Eph. 1:17–23), and to move to a place in history where sin is destroyed (1 Cor. 15:20–28; Rev. 21:3–5) and a new/renewed creation replaces it.

As we outlined in the last lesson, sin is a choice away from life and a path toward death. Jesus died to experience the death we first chose for us. He died taking our sin on himself. He offers us an exchange—His life for our sin.

Types of Personal Salvation

The Bible talks about three stages of salvation as it relates to the individual. Theologians use the words justification, sanctification, and glorification as a way of describing these stages of salvation.

Dear friends, we are already God's children, but he has not yet shown us what we will be like when Christ appears. But we do know that we will be like him, for we will see him as he is. And all who have this eager expectation will keep themselves pure, just as he is pure. 1 John 3:3

Justification: This refers to the moment in time that we are made right with God. It not only refers to the past event (Christ's suffering, death, resurrection) but to the moment we receive that work for ourselves, as seen in the next session on receiving salvation (Rom. 5:1, 8:15–17).

Sanctification: This refers to the potential for ongoing progressive transformation inside that frees us from our propensity to sin. We have a choice to yield to the ongoing work of God in our lives

(John 10:10; Rom. 6:16–22; Heb. 2:15).

Glorification: This refers to the final stage of salvation that affects our bodies and our souls. This is the final stage of salvation that promises recreated bodies and renewed mind, motives, and emotions (John 3:16; 1 Cor. 15:52). This stage also refers to the moment when God will set everything right; evil will be destroyed in the world, and God will create a new world for us to experience (Rom. 5:9; 1 Thess. 1:10; Rev. 22).

DISCUSSION

In your own words, describe the difference between justification, sanctification, and glorification.

_____

_____

_____

Explain how God is currently working in your life to make you more like Jesus.

_____

_____

_____

Personal Application

_____

_____

_____

_____

_____

CHAPTER NOTES:

See Appendix for Q&A

BIBLE STORYLINE

The Bible is a complete story from beginning to end.

CHAPTER 26

GETTING ORIENTED

BIG IDEA

The Bible is a connected story. Once you understand the framework and the main plot, you will begin to see its theme from cover to cover. You will also start to see other connected sub-plots, stories, and themes. It's like putting together a giant puzzle. First you build the outside edges and then slowly build inward.

THOUGHTS

Let's start by looking at the Bible bookends. Open the Bible to Genesis 2-3 at the beginning and compare it to Revelation 22 at the end. Let's first read the chapters and focus on some of the following verses. There's no doubt you will spot similar ideas in both sections.

Genesis 2 - 3

Then the Lord God planted a garden in Eden in the east, and there he placed the man he had made. The Lord God made all sorts of trees grow up from the ground—trees that were beautiful and that produced delicious fruit. In the middle of the garden, He placed the tree of life and the tree of the knowledge of good and evil. A river flowed from the land of Eden, watering the garden and then dividing it into four branches. (3:17) And to the man, he said, "Since you listened to your wife and ate from the tree whose fruit I commanded you not to eat, the ground is cursed because of you ...

Revelation 22

Then the angel showed me a river with the water of life, clear as crystal, flowing from the throne of God and of the Lamb. It flowed down the center of the main street. On each side of the river grew a tree of life, bearing twelve crops of fruit, with fresh produce each month. The leaves were used for medicine to heal the nations. No longer will there be a curse upon anything. For the throne of God and the Lamb will be there, and his servants will worship him.

Did you notice in both a garden, a river, a tree of life, and a curse instilled and removed? What are they, and what do you think they mean? They are the beginning and end of the story, which has five parts.

- Section 1—The Beginnings: In this section (Genesis 1–11), we will read about a period covering two thousand years in which God creates the world (PURPOSE), humanity rejects God (SIN), but God sets into place a plan to restore creation (SALVATION).

- Section 2—Israel: In the second section (Genesis 12 – Malachi), we will read about the shaping of God's SALVATION plan through the family of Israel, and the FAITH required to get in on it.

- Section 3—Jesus: In this section (Matthew – John), we will see the climax of the SALVATION plan as Jesus overcomes SIN.

- Section 4—Church: In this section (Acts – Jude), we will see how FAITH accesses SALVATION and how the main message begins to expand throughout the world.

- Section 5—Future: In this section (Revelation), we will see how God is restoring the world to its intended state.

CHAPTER NOTES:

See Appendix for Q&A

CHAPTER 27

BEGINNINGS

CREATION	SIN	SALVATION
God creates the world with purpose and humanity as leaders. We are able to fulfil purpose as we obey God. (Gen 1:26, 2:24)	We reject God's authority. Sin enters the world. It affects everything: health, relationships, the earth, work, etc (Gen 3)	God sets in motion a plan to restore humanity to its created purpose. (Gen 3:15)

FLOOD	DISPERSION
Sin increases so much that God wipes out humanity through a worldwide flood. Noah and his family are saved. (Gen 6:10)	Humanity multiplies and God confuses their language and disperses people groups throughout the earth. (Gen 11)

The first eleven chapters of Genesis summarize two thousand years of history: the Garden of Eden, the multiplication of humanity, the worldwide flood, the formation of city-states, and the dispersion of people throughout the earth. In the first few chapters, key ideas emerge. These ideas are central to the main message.

CREATION—Genesis 1–2

God creates everything. He creates each realm: the natural, the spiritual, the eternal, and the separation realm. He creates all creatures. He creates angels and demons. He creates us.

SIN—Genesis 3

Humanity obeys Satan and disobeys God. Sin is introduced into our world.

SALVATION—Genesis 3:15

God promises redemption from sin and its effects.

THE FLOOD—Genesis 6–10

Sin increases. It destroys God's good creation. God sends a worldwide flood to wipe out creation. A new world emerges with eight human beings who are saved to begin again.

BABEL—Genesis 11

People multiply in the earth and attempt to accumulate resources and power. God disperses people to repopulate the earth.

DISCUSSION

In the first eleven chapters of Genesis, a variety of questions emerge. It's essential to walk through these questions with someone who is able to help you answer them. List them here.

Personal Application

CHAPTER NOTES:

See Appendix for Q&A

CHAPTER 28

ISRAEL

PATRIARCHS	EGYPT	WILDERNESS
God chooses a family to bring salvation to the world. The family becomes a nation. Abraham > Isaac > Jacob > 12 Tribes. Genesis 12-45	The nation is enslaved for 400 years. Israel is freed from slavery. Genesis 46 – Exodus 15	The law, temple worship and social hierarchy established. The nation wanders for 40 years. Exodus 16 – Deuteronomy 34
NEW LAND	**KINGS**	**DIVISION**
Joshua leads the Israelites in conquest of Canaan. He is succeeded by other judges including Samson and Deborah. Joshua ¬1 – Judges 21	The nation of Israel implements authoritarian government under a king. Saul, David and Solomon are the first three kings. 1 Samuel, 2 Samuel, Psalms, Proverbs, Ecclesiastes, Song of Songs	Solomon's sons divide the kingdom: ten northern tribes under Jeroboam, and two southern tribes led by Rehoboam. 1 & 2 Kings, 1 & 2 Chronicles Isaiah, Hosea, Joel, Amos, Obadiah, Jonah, Micah
DISPERSION CAPTIVITY	**RETURN**	**SILENCE**
Ten northern tribes are dispersed by war. Two southern tribes are exiled to Babylon/Persia. Jeremiah, Lamentations, Ezekiel, Daniel, Nahum, Habakkuk, Zephaniah	The southern tribes return in two stages under Zerubbabel and Nehemiah. Esther, Ezra, Nehemiah, Haggai, Zechariah, Malachi	During four hundred years of prophetic silence, the nation of Israel comes under the control of the Roman empire.

Genesis 12 to Malachi summarizes two thousand years of history of the Nation of Israel.

The Patriarchs

God sovereignly chooses Abraham and his descendants through whom to redeem humanity (Gen. 12:3). God also promises to protect and provide for Abrahams's descendants on the way (Gen. 12:1–3, 17:1–8, 22:17). God chooses Jacob (Abraham's grandson) through whom to keep His promise. God appears to Jacob several times and changes his name to Israel (Gen. 35:10–13).

Egypt and Wilderness

The family of Israel providentially moves from Canaan to Egypt but become slaves to the Egyptians for four hundred years (Gen. 15:13, 45:1–11; Exod. 1:8–14). God raises up Moses to lead the nation out of slavery and help set up the legal, economic, and religious system in the wilderness (Exod. 3:4–14, 19:1–8, 20:1–34:35), including the Tabernacle (Exod. 25–30) and the Law (Exod. 20).

New Land and Kings

The nation of Israel goes back to Canaan to possess their land (read Josh. 1–8). God raises a series of leaders to help keep the country free from conquest (book of Judges). The people want a king, and God raises up three great Kings: Saul, David, and Solomon.

Division, Dispersion, Captivity, and Return

After Solomon's death, the kingdom divides into the Northern (ten tribes at Bethel) and Southern Kingdom (Judah/Benjamin at Jerusalem). The Northern Kingdom is dismantled and dispersed under Assyria. The Southern Kingdom goes through a period of captivity and exile in Babylon and Persia (1 Sam. 1–3, 8–10, 15–17; 2 Sam. 5, 7; 1 Kings 6–12; 2 Kings 17, 24). Through the leadership of Zerubbabel and Nehemiah, they ultimately return to Israel and rebuild the city and the temple.

Throughout the Old Testament, God sends prophets to help

bring correction and hope to His people. He continues to confirm His promise to Abraham about redeeming humanity through prophets like Samuel (2 Sam. 14:14), David (2 Sam. 7:1–16, Ps. 22), Isaiah (Isa. 9:6–7, 53), Jeremiah (Jer. 23:5, 33:15), Mic. (Micah 5:2), and Zech. (Zechariah 9:9).

Silence

A period of four hundred years separates Malachi and the arrival of Jesus.

DISCUSSION

How do you feel about the idea that the entire Old Testament centres on the story of the nation of Israel?

Discuss other questions about the nation of Israel here.

Personal Application

CHAPTER NOTES:

_____

_____

_____

_____

_____

_____

_____

_____

_____

_____

_____

_____

_____

_____

_____

_____

_____

See Appendix for Q&A

CHAPTER 29

JESUS

PROMISED	BIRTH	LIFE
Jesus' life fulfilled over four hundred prophecies in the Jewish scriptures	Jesus is supernaturally conceived, born in Bethlehem, and raised in Nazareth in a large Jewish family.	At age 30 He begins travelling and teaching for 3 years along with 12 disciples. He teaches on God's kingdom, heals every type of disease, exercises power over nature, calls people to repent, put their trust in God.

DEATH	RESURRECTION	COMMISSION AND ASCENSION
Jesus is falsely accused, condemned, suffers torture, and is sentenced to a criminal's death on a cross.	Jesus rises from the dead and is seen by five hundred witnesses.	Jesus commissions His followers to make disciples of people throughout the world. He ascends into heaven with a promise to return.

Promised

Jesus's arrival is prophesied in Jewish Scriptures. There are over four hundred prophecies about Him.

From outside sources, we know that Jesus lived between the dates of 3 BC and 35 AD. He had a sibling named James and an active following. He was called Messiah, and because of that, He was not liked by the Jewish leaders. He was eventually executed by the Roman government between 25–35 AD.

Birth

The biblical narrative tells us that Mary, a virgin, supernaturally conceives Jesus (Isa. 7:14; Matt. 1:18, 20, 23; Luke 1:27, 34). Jesus is born in Bethlehem (Luke 2) and raised in Nazareth in a traditional Jewish home.

Life

We know that Jesus has a large family of brothers, sisters, and cousins (Matt. 13:55; Mark 3:31; Acts 1:14), and that He works alongside his father as a carpenter. At thirty years of age, Jesus is baptized in the Jordan River by John the Baptist (Matt. 3:13–14). He begins a travelling and teaching ministry for three years, going no more than two hundred miles from where He was born.

Death, Resurrection, Ascension

Jesus is falsely accused and condemned, suffers torture, and dies a criminal's death on a cross at thirty-three years of age (Matt. 27:29–43). He rises from the dead three days later and is seen alive by over five hundred people (1 Cor. 15:6). Forty days later, He ascends into heaven (Acts 1:9–12).

God & Man: Jesus Is Fully Man and Fully God

As a man, Jesus experiences human limitations such as hunger and thirst (Matt. 4:2) and tiredness (John 4:6), emotions such as anger and sorrow (Mark 11:12–25; John 11), and physical pain (Matt. 27:29–43).

Jesus also exhibits the character and nature of God as a human being, exercising God's power over nature (Luke 4:31–36, 5:1–11, 7:24–30), disease (John 4:43–54), evil spirits (Luke 4:31–36, 7:24–30), and death (Luke 7:13–16, John 11). He defines and forgives sin (Mark 2:7–11) and reveals people's thoughts and motives (Mark 2:8). He expresses extraordinary love and grace (Luke 19:10; John 8) and accurately predicts His suffering, death, and resurrection (Matt. 16:21, 20:17–10; Luke 9:21).

The Main Message

Jesus taught that He existed outside of it all, as God, and had come to earth as a human being to explain life and remove sin for now and in eternity (John 5:18, 8:58, 10:30–33, 14:9). Jesus's invitation to humanity was to follow Him (Luke 9:23–25), learn from Him (Matt. 11:29), look to Him as the source of life who has come to die for our sin (John 3:16, 8:23–28), and live for Him, making Him the centre of one's life (Matt. 28:18–20).

DISCUSSION

What is your view of Jesus?

Do you have any challenges with Jesus's teachings?

Personal Application

CHAPTER NOTES:

See Appendix for Q&A

CHAPTER 30

THE CHURCH

START	PERSECUTION AND DISPERSION
Followers of Jesus begin to multiply as a result of the Holy Spirit and the witness of the early church. Acts 1–7	The disciples are persecuted and scattered from Jerusalem. Many move to Antioch of Syria and other Jewish communities throughout the Roman Empire Acts 8–12

CHURCH PLANTING	100 AD TO PRESENT
The first wave of mission work and gentile (non-Jewish) churches are started because of Paul and Barnabas. Acts 13–28 Romans – Jude	In the last two thousand years the church has multiplied and divided into different groups with particular emphasis: Catholic, Orthodox, Protestant, etc.

Jesus's followers are commissioned by Him (Acts 1:8) and empowered by the Spirit (Acts 2) to reach their world. The church in Jerusalem grows daily (Acts 2:42–47) as it branches away as a sect of Judaism. Due to persecution (Acts 8:1), Jesus's followers disperse to Judea and Samaria. New churches begin in Tyre, Sidon, Ptolemais, Cyprus, and Syria.

Through an influential church in Antioch of Syria (modern Antakya, Turkey), the first missionary church planters begin to reach Jewish settlements abroad. Paul and others take missionary church planting trips through Asia and Europe. The early non-Jewish believers convert through Paul and Peter's (Acts 10) influence. The church then experiences periods of expansion and persecution. The book of Acts to the book of Jude cover history from 30 to 70 AD. First, Second, Third John and the book of Revelation are generally dated from 90 to 95 AD.

DISCUSSION

What about the early church is attractive to you?

_____

_____

_____

How does the early church compare to the church today? Why do you think that is?

_____

_____

_____

Personal Application

_____

_____

_____

_____

_____

CHAPTER NOTES:

See Appendix for Q&A

CHAPTER 31

THE FUTURE

TRIBULATION	JESUS'S RETURN	JUDGEMENT
Pain and evil in the world	A literal and physical return to our world. God will take over. Sin and pain will be removed.	Those who have accepted Jesus will be with Him. Those who reject Jesus will be removed.

FINAL DESTINATION	THREE VIEWS
A new existence in a new heaven & earth.	Premillennialism – we are on the journey towards the end

Postmillennialism – we are in the midst of the end

Amillennialism – we live in an endless cycle of the end |

God is moving history to a future that He has planned since the beginning. There are dozens of passages in the Old Testament, the words of Jesus, the letters to the early church, and the book of Revelation that help articulate what this will look like. Those studying what the Bible teaches about the future (eschatology) see a concentration of passages focusing on the following significant concepts.

Tribulation

We will experience a growing period of evil and pain that affects our world (Matt. 24; 2 Thess. 2; 2 Pet. 3:1–15; Rev. 8–9, 16).

Jesus's Return to Earth:

Jesus will return to earth literally and physically, and we will forever be with Him (Matt. 24:30; Acts 1:11; 1 Thess. 4:13–18; 2 Thess. 2:1–2; Rev. 19:11–12). There are signs of this return, but God only knows the timing (Matt. 24; Mark 13; Luke 21; 2 Tim. 3; 2 Pet. 3:1–10).

Judgement:

God will take over our world, bring peace, remove Satan, and establish His rule (Dan. 7–9; Rev. 11:15–18; 21:1–22:21). All who have accepted God will be with Him, and those who reject God will be removed (Dan. 12:2; Matt. 13:41–42, 25:41–46; Heb. 10:26–31; 2 Pet. 2:4; Rev. 20:10–15, 21:8).

Final Destination

There will be a new heaven and a new earth (Isa. 65:17; 2 Pet. 3:13; Rev. 21–22). We will be forever with Jesus, free from sin and pain (Rev. 21:3–4). We will be recreated with new physical bodies (1 Cor. 15; Phil. 3:21; Col. 3:10; 2 Pet. 1), we will be given rest-filled roles by God (Matt. 25:14–34; Rev. 22:3), and we will walk in new types of relationships (Luke 20:34–36). We will be able to experience new life as it was meant to be lived.

It is important to note that there are three significant theological perspectives, with several variations of each perspective on these future concepts. While studying these perspectives go beyond the scope of this study, they are known as amillennialism, post-millennialism, and pre-millennialism.

DISCUSSION

How do you feel about the idea that Jesus will return to earth?

Discuss other questions that you have.

Personal Application

CHAPTER NOTES:

See Appendix for Q&A

YOUR NEXT STEP

This is not the end of the journey. It's merely the beginning of a whole new life of discovery. Here are two ways that you can continue to grow in your faith.

1. Find and commit to a church where you can build relationships, grow in your faith, and contribute through volunteering.
2. Join a Bible class, a small group, or get involved in serving on a team. You will connect and grow with others.

APPENDIX

CHAPTER 1 – MESSAGE

Q & A

AREN'T ALL RELIGIONS THE SAME? DON'T THEY ALL TELL US TO BE GOOD, AND IF WE ARE, WE WILL GO TO AN AFTERLIFE?

While many religions share similar ethics, such as peace and love, they all have exclusive claims about how one obtains salvation and who is responsible for it. Christians believe that Jesus is the only one who can offer us salvation. He freely offers salvation by grace to those who put their faith in Him.

DOES GOD SEND PEOPLE WHO DON'T ACCEPT JESUS TO HELL? IF SO, HOW CAN HE BE LOVING?

Since God is the source of life, the moment we walk away from Him, we experience less and less life. Since God is also the source of love, H e allows us to experience the ends of our decision. If we choose to walk away from Him, we are the ones who decide on an afterlife without Him. If He would step in and intervene and force us to be with Him, He would not be loving .

WHY IS THERE EVIL IN THE WORLD?

Love requires choice. Since God is loving, He gives us and others the freedom to hurt each other. We are promised ul-timate justice in eternity and that God can create good from the evil we create. God also gives us the freedom to make our world better and asks that we do our part to make this world a better place.

HOW ABOUT PEOPLE WHO NEVER HAD A CHANCE TO HEAR THE MESSAGE?

It's impossible to know if a person has heard the message of Jesus or not in their lifetime. There are many different stories of people to whom Jesus has personally appeared (Acts 9:1–4). The good news is that God has a history of responding to people who want to know Him (Acts 10). We also find the promise that God reveals Himself to every person in different ways (Rom. 1:19–20).

CHAPTER 2 – BAPTISM

Q & A

CAN I GET BAPTIZED AT HOME?

Baptism was intended as a public sign of what God has done in one's life. Baptism does not save us. Baptism can take place in any body of water where one makes a public declaration of faith. This can be at home, in a lake, or at church in front of your friends and family.

IF I HAVE BEEN BAPTIZED ALREADY, SHOULD I GET BAPTIZED AGAIN?

Some people who have already been baptized and then walked away from faith in Jesus like to get rebaptized as a sign of their recommitment to Him. While it's not necessary to get rebaptized, there's no rule against it. The key is to remember that baptism does not save you but reflects what God is doing in your life.

WHAT IS THE DIFFERENCE BETWEEN SPRINKLING AND IMMERSION BAPTISM?

Different Christian traditions practice different methods of being baptized, whether it's sprinkling, pouring, or full submersion. The earliest record suggests total immersion was the preferred method for the early church but allowed for pouring, where total immersion was not possible. In 1311, a church council held in Ravenna declared immersion, pouring, and sprinkling as all equally valid. Since then, some traditions have held to that position while other traditions do not .

CHAPTER 3 – SPIRIT

GIFTS OF THE HOLY SPIRIT

Motivational (practical) gifts (Rom. 12:3–7):

- Every Christian can operate in at least one spiritual gift (1 Pet. 4:10). No one can operate in every gift (1 Cor. 12:28–30). God chooses what flows through us (1 Cor. 12:7–11). Love is the heartbeat of all gifts (1 Cor. 13:1–3). Gifts can only be expressed with others around us (1 Cor. 12:27).

- Service: the special God-given desire and ability to identify the needs of the church and find resources to fill those needs (Acts 6:1–7; Rom. 12:7; Gal. 6:2,10; 2 Tim. 1:16–18; Titus 3:14)

- Exhortation: the special God-given desire and ability to encourage and help people, no matter their situation (pain or rebellion), to embrace God's will (Acts 14:22; Rom. 12:8; 1 Tim. 4:13; Heb. 10:25)

- Giving: the special God-given desire and ability to obtain and contribute material goods, over and above tithes and resources, to the church with cheerfulness (Mark 12:41–44; Rom. 12:8; 2 Cor. 8:1–7, 9:2–8)

- Leadership: the special God-given desire and ability to see God's will in a situation and then organize, assemble, and guide a team to accomplish that will collectively (Acts 7:10, 15:7–11; Rom. 12:8; 1 Tim. 5:17; Heb. 13:17)

- Mercy: the special God-given desire and ability to feel genuine compassion for individuals in physical, mental, or emotional problems and do things that reflect Christ's love to them (Matt. 20:29–34, 25:34–40; Mark 9:41; Luke 10:33–35; Acts 11:28–30, 16:33–34; Rom. 12:8)

- Helps: the special God-given desire and ability to practically serve felt physical needs of individuals in the body, enabling others to be effective in their spiritual gifts (Mark 15:40–41; Luke 8:2–3; Acts 9:36; Rom. 16:1–2; 1 Cor. 12:28;)

- Administration: the special God-given desire and ability to organize and set in place effective plans to ensure the smooth operation of an assembly (Luke 14:28–30; Acts 6:1–7; 1 Cor. 12:28).

Ministry (functional) gifts (Eph. 4:11):

- Some operate in these gifts, whether they have the position of an overseer, elder, or deacon in a local church (1 Tim. 3:1; Titus 1).

- Apostle: a person sent by another; a messenger; envoy, one sent. There are three views here. Some believe that only the first twelve disciples and Paul (who replaced Judas) held the position of an Apostle. Others believe that apostleship is a position that is passed down in succession from Peter/James on. Others argue that those who are called in church planting or mission work can also be considered modern-day apostles.

- Prophet: a person God chooses to use to speak a clear message to a specific person/group that "forth tells." They remind us of something God has already spoken in His Word, bring encouragement and clarity, and help identify spiritual gifts. In some cases, God gives them an awareness of future events. We see prophets in the early church in Acts 7:54, 17:32–34, 21:9–10, 26:24–29; 1 Thess. 1:5; 1 Cor.14:1,3.

- Evangelist: a "publisher of glad tidings." This special God-given desire and ability allow certain members to share the gospel with unbelievers in such a way that more people than average become disciples and mature members of the body of Christ. They have a burning desire to see people come to faith and will spend most of their time speaking to people about Christ (Acts 8:5–6, 26-40, 14:21, 21:8; Eph. 4:11–14; 2 Tim. 4:5).

- Pastor : a shepherd of people. This special God-given desire and ability allow certain members to assume long term personal responsibility for the spiritual welfare of people. They help guide, teach, correct, pray, encourage, and much more (John 10:1–18; Eph. 4:11–14; 1 Tim. 3:1–7; 1 Pet. 5:1–3).

- Teacher: a conveyor and clarifier of God's Word. This special God-given desire and ability allow certain members to communicate the truth of the Word of God effectively (Acts 18:11–14, 20:20–21 Rom. 12:7; 1 Cor. 12:28; Eph. 4:11–14).

Manifestation (charismatic) gifts (1 Cor. 12:1–12, 28):

- Gifts are to be desired and regularly activated (1 Cor. 14:1, 39; 1 Thess. 5:19; 1 Tim. 4:14; 2 Tim. 1:6).

- Wisdom: This is the spiritual gift in which the Spirit empowers Christians with a supernatural understanding and biblical application in difficult situations where information is lacking and no clear answer is possible (1 Cor. 2:6; 2 Cor. 1:12; James 3:13–17).

- Knowledge: This is the spiritual gift in which the Spirit transmits His specific knowledge to you about something that you would have no ability or means to know about with your limited intelligence and insight (1 Cor. 2:11).

- Discernment (of spirits): This is the spiritual gift in which the Spirit enables certain Christians to know without a doubt whether a statement or behaviour is of God, Satan, or man (Acts 5:3–6, 16:16–18; 1 Cor. 12:10; 1 John 4:1).

- Prophecy: This is the spiritual gift in which God shares a message through us to a group or individual. This message reflects the character, attitude, and motivation of God ("But he who prophesies speaks edification and exhortation and comfort to men," (1 Cor. 14:4). This gift is available for everyone to operate in (1 Cor. 14:31, 39 – "you can all prophesy"). We are encouraged to desire it (1 Cor. 14:1– "desire spiritual gifts, especially the gift of prophecy") and learn to operate in it. We are to properly test all prophecy that we receive, as there are always false prophets and well-meaning believers speaking out of their imaginations. ("Do not despise prophecies, but test everything; hold fast what is good"– 1 Thess. 5:20–21.)

- Tongues: This spiritual gift is a prayer language that can be activated privately (1 Cor. 14:2, 14–15; Eph. 6:18; Jude 1:20). It is also the gift of giving a divine message in a language unknown to the speaker but possibly known by the hearer. It may require spiritual interpretation (1 Cor. 12:11).

- Interpretation: This is the God-given ability to understand prophecies and tongues and help discern and apply their meaning in context (1 Thess. 5:20–21).

- Faith: This is the God-given ability to act in a way that sees great things happening despite circumstances that suggest an impossibility. This is rooted in our growing faith (Eph. 2:8–9) but moves beyond the possible to the impossible (Matt. 17:20; Acts 3:1–10; Heb. 11).

- Healing and Miracles: This is the special God-given de-sire and ability to serve as human intermediaries through whom God will cure others and perform powerful acts that are perceived by observers to have altered the ordinary course of nature. There seem to be several types of gifts of healing and miracles for different diseases (Acts 3:1–10, 5:12–16, 9:32–40, 19:11–12, 20:7–12; 1 Cor. 12:9, 10, 28; Rom. 15:18–19).

CHAPTER 4 – QUIET TIME

Q & A

DO I NEED TO SET ASIDE A ROOM IN MY HOUSE TO TALK TO GOD?

You can, but it's not required. God doesn't hear you more if you do. He can connect with you no matter where you are and when you spend time with Him.

IF I SPEND MORE TIME WITH GOD, WILL I GET CLOSER TO HIM?

Our relationship with God grows as we spend time with Him. While there may be times when we take extended time alone with Him, we're not created as hermits. We also grow close to God as we spend time with people who are close to Him too.

WHAT IF I MISS A DAY?

As you walk with God, there may be days when you miss unin-terrupted alone time with Him. This behaviour doesn't make God love you any less or put you at risk of bad things happening. As we grow closer to God, we will desire more and more time with Him.

QUIET TIME JOURNAL

	Scripture	Prayer	Thoughts
Monday			
Tuesday			
Wednesday			
Thursday			
Friday			
Saturday			
Sunday			

CHAPTER 5 – PRAYER

Q & A

HOW LONG SHOULD I PRAY?

There are no minimum time requirements in the Bible. Prayer is talking to God, not a formula to get what you want. It can happen at different times each day (Dan. 6:10-28) or all at once.

HOW DO I KNOW THAT GOD WILL HEAR MY PRAYER?

God always answers prayer, but He may not always answer our prayer as we want Him to. If you begin writing down your prayers in a journal and date them when the prayer is answered, you'll grow in your faith. Sometimes when a prayer isn't answered, it reveals that God has another plan or is trying to teach us something.

I DON'T THINK I CAN PRAY PUBLICLY AS WELL AS OTHERS DO.

Sometimes we hear other people pray and think that we need to use the flowery language that they do. Prayer is about being yourself and genuinely connecting with God. You don't need to use a special language. Some people articulate very well publicly. Some people don't. God responds to the heart (Luke 18:9–14).

HOW DO I HEAR GOD'S VOICE?

We first become aware of God's voice through little nudges to stop or proceed with our words or actions. As we read the Bible, certain Bible passages will come back to us. As we pray for God to give us wisdom, we will be given a way forward. We become more aware of God's direction with time.

CHAPTER 6 – READING THE BIBLE

BIBLE READING PLAN

Hebrew Writings (Old Testament)

__ Genesis 1:1–3:19	The creation and fall of humanity
__ Genesis 12, 28:10–15; 32:22–28	The making of the nation of Israel
__ Genesis 37, 39–46	The story of Joseph
__ Exodus 1–6	The story of Moses
__ Exodus 7–14	Moses and Pharaoh
__ Exodus 19:1–20:21	The 10 Commandments
__ Deuteronomy 6:1–7:26, 11:13–21	Obedience from love
__ Judges 1:1–2:19	Cycles of disobedience
__ 1 Samuel 7–9, 15–17	Saul and David
__ 2 Samuel 5, 7–9, 11–12	Stories of David's life
__ 1 Kings 2–3, 6, 11	Solomon the king
__ 1 Kings 11:9–14:31	Division of the nation
__ 1 Kings 17–19; 2 Kings 2, 4	Elijah and Elisha
__ Job 1–2, 38–42	Job
__ Psalm 1, 19, 23, 139	Favourite Psalms 1
__ Psalm 6, 22, 38, 51	Favourite Psalms 2
__ Proverbs 3, 16, 5, 7 & 31	Wisdom
__ Isaiah 9:6–7, 53	The promise of Jesus
__ Jeremiah 11–12, 23, 31	The new covenant
__ Jonah 1–4	Jonah
__ Daniel 1–3	Exile in Babylon
__ Daniel 4–6	Daniel
__ Hosea 1–2	God's plan for His people
__ Nehemiah 1–2, 4–5, 8–9	Rebuilding Jerusalem
__ Esther 1–8	Esther

Christian Writings (New Testament)

__ John 1:1–18	Jesus as God
__ Luke 1–2	Jesus's birth story
__ Luke 4:14–44	Jesus begins His ministry
__ Matthew 5–6	Jesus teaches how to live
__ John 3	Jesus reveals God's plan
__ John 5	Jesus's miracles
__ John 11	Jesus's power over death
__ John 15	Staying connected to Jesus
__ Matthew 26–27	Jesus's arrest and crucifixion
__ John 20, Luke 24	Jesus's resurrection & ascension
__ Acts 2	The Holy Spirit
__ Acts 9, 16–19	Saul becoming Paul
__ Acts 10–11	The first non-Jewish Christians
__ Romans 3	Sin, faith, salvation
__ Romans 7–8	Our fight against sin
__ 1 Corinthians 13; Ephesians 5	Love as the goal
__ 1 Corinthians 15	Eternal life
__ Galatians 2:15–3:14;	Freedom in Jesus
__ Galatians 5	The fruit of the flesh and spirit
__ Ephesians 6	The armour of God
__ Philippians 1:18–2:18	The role of humility
__ Hebrews 1, 11	Jesus and faith
__ James 1, 1 Peter 1	Good works
__ 1 John 4	God is Love
__ Revelation 21–22	The new heaven and earth

CHAPTER 15 – CHURCH

Q&A

HOW DO I KNOW WHEN GOD IS LEADING ME TO LEAVE THE CHURCH I ATTEND?

While it's important to be faithful to a local group of believers at the church you attend, on some occasions one should consider leaving a local church. All churches are made of imperfect people, so all churches will have challenges. When the challenges become insurmountable, it may be good to move on. These challenges may include bad theology, spiritual abuse, or illegal activities.

I HAVE A PROBLEM WITH HOW MY CHURCH SPENDS MONEY. WHAT SHOULD I DO ABOUT IT?

You could connect with members of your church board who help to oversee the finances and share your thoughts with them. You must differentiate between opinion (such as they spent too much on lights) and best practices.

HOW DO I FIND OUT WHERE I SHOULD GET INVOLVED IN MY CHURCH?

Just start by serving in an area that interests you. As you begin to serve, you will naturally find what you enjoy and where you best fit. Take a spiritual gifts test; it will also help you narrow down how you can serve.

SHOULD I BE DONATING MONEY TO MY CHURCH OR ANOTHER MINISTRY LOCALLY/OVERSEAS THAT SEEMS TO ALSO HAVE NEED?

When you join a church, you take on the responsibility of the finances required for the church to operate. Once you are confident you're doing your part, it's always good to support others as well.

I WAS HURT IN A CHURCH, SO NOW I DON'T WANT TO GET INVOLVED IN ONE.

Many people have been hurt by church leaders and the words and actions of other followers of Jesus. As a result, they're hesitant to commit to a group. Other Christians have also shared the truth in a way that others couldn't digest. As a result of not liking what they were told, they discounted the church altogether. It's important to see the difference between other-imposed and self-imposed hurt. It's important to receive the truth, even when it hurts. It's important not to discount the whole church as a result of rogue members. Yet one should never subject themselves to spiritual abuse.

CHAPTER 18

The Life and Times of Jesus the Messiah by Alfred Edersheim, and the work of late Professor Emeritus of Science at Westmont College, Peter Stoner, in Science Speaks, illustrate that the chance of one person fulfilling these prophecies is 1 in 10^157 (10 with 157 zeros behind it). This formula creates a mathematical chance of probability of truthfulness that is unmatched anywhere. Here are a sample of prophecies that were fulfilled in Jesus.

Jesus would be born in Bethlehem.	Micah 5:2	Matthew 2:1 Luke 2:4-6
Jesus would be born of a virgin.	Isaiah 7:14	Matthew 1:22-23 Luke 1:26-31
Jesus would spend a season in Egypt.	Hosea 11:1	Matthew 2:14-15
A massacre of children would happen at Jesus's birthplace.	Jeremiah 31:15	Matthew 2:16-18
Jesus would be called a Nazarene.	Isaiah 11:1	Matthew 2:23
Jesus would bring light to Galilee.	Isaiah 9:1-2	Matthew 4:13-16
Jesus would speak in parables.	Psalm 78:2-4 Isaiah 6:9-10	Matthew 13:10-15, 34-35
Jesus would be called King.	Psalm 2:6 Zechariah 9:9	Matthew 27:37 Mark 11:7-11
Jesus would be betrayed.	Psalm 41:9 Zechariah 11:12-13	Luke 22:47-48 Matthew 26:14-16
Jesus's price money would be used to buy a potter's field.	Zechariah 11:12-13	Matthew 27:9-10
Jesus would be hated without cause.	Psalm 35:19 Psalm 69:4	John 15:24-25
Jesus would be crucified with criminals.	Isaiah 53:12	Matthew 27:38 Mark 15:27-28
Jesus would be given vinegar to drink.	Psalm 69:21	Matthew 27:34 John 19:28-30

Jesus's hands and feet would be pierced.	Psalm 22:16 Zechariah 12:10	John 20:25-27
Jesus would be mocked and ridiculed.	Psalm 22:7-8	Luke 23:35
Soldiers would gamble for Jesus's garments.	Psalm 22:18	Luke 23:34 Matthew 27:35-36
Jesus's bones would not be broken.	Exodus 12:46 Psalm 34:20	John 19:33-36
Jesus would pray for his enemies.	Psalm 109:4	Luke 23:34
Soldiers would pierce Jesus's side.	Zechariah 12:10	John 19:34
Jesus would be buried with the rich.	Isaiah 53:9	Matthew 27:57-60
Jesus would rise from the dead.	Psalm 16:10 Psalm 49:15	Matthew 28:2-7 Acts 2:22-32

Q&A

HOW DO WE KNOW THE BIBLE WASN'T CHANGED ALONG THE WAY TO CONTROL THE MASSES?

Some people suggest that there have been different times since Jesus, that people in power changed the content of the Bible. That suggestion isn't logical. The earliest biblical manuscripts were written in various languages and found in different parts of the world that no single political empire has ever had access to. It would have been much easier to burn copies of the Bible rather than rewrite entire manuscripts by hand. The existence of primary sources from different languages and cultures that align is evidence to the contrary.

IS THE APOCRYPHA PART OF THE BIBLE? WHY OR WHY NOT?

These books were written between 100 and 200 BC but were never accepted by the early Jewish leaders. The early Christian community varied on their views of the Apocrypha because of their authors, contradictions, and exclusion from the Hebrew version of the Old Testament. In some regions church councils accepted the books and in other regions church leaders did not. As a result of some in the Protestant reformation that rejected the works, the Apocrypha was formally canonized by the Roman Catholic church at the Ecumenical Council of Trent in 1546. Currently, the Roman Catholic and Orthodox Church recognize the apocrypha as scripture and Protestant denominations do not.

CHAPTER 22

Q&A

DO I NEED TO FEAR DEMONS COMING TO LIVE IN ME?

While demons can cause opposition and spiritual attack externally, followers of Jesus do not need to fear demons coming to live inside of them (2 Cor. 6:15–16; Col. 1:13; 1 Pet. 1:5; 1 John 5:18). en God's good creation, He must step in to ensure its ultimate preservation.

CHAPTER 27

Q&A

WHY IS THE DEVIL A SNAKE?

Not all snakes have the devil and demons living in them. In the Bible, demons entered the bodies of other animals (Matthew 8) to interact with humans. We're not told why the devil chose to use a snake in this story. Remember that the story is written in a poetic format to articulate a more profound truth.

HOW DOES EVOLUTION FIT INTO GENESIS 1?

Macroevolution is a theory espoused by some scientists and opposed by others. Similarly, some theologians advocate for creation days to take place over an extended period, as in evolutionary theory. Other theologians suggest that the Hebrew writing style only allows for literal days, and Jesus's affirmation of creation supports a literal seven-day creation (Mark 10:6; John 5:45–47 with Exod. 20:11).

DID GOD FLOOD THE ENTIRE WORLD? WHY?

Jesus and the early disciples taught that the entire world flooded, not just a small part of it (Matt. 24:37–39; Luke 17:26–27, Heb. 11:7; 1 Pet. 3:20; 2 Pet. 2:5, 3:6). When anything begins to threaten God's good creation, He must step in to ensure its ultimate preservation.

WHY DIDN'T GOD HAVE JESUS COME AT THE BEGINNING?

How could God demonstrate His love for humanity and allow us to eagerly desire Him without also allowing us to experience the ends of our decision and the process of restoration rather than just a moment of recovery? Perhaps our affection for Him mattered more than our comfort (2 Pet. 3:9).

ABOUT THE AUTHOR

JONATHAN GALLO

Jonathan Gallo's greatest passion is to see the multiplication of discipleship-first churches that help new believers grow and mature into leaders who help others do the same.

Jonathan grew up in Toronto's multicultural neighborhoods, where he was exposed to various beliefs. Amid all the options, he reconfirmed his early faith while attending the University of Toronto and felt the call to full-time ministry. He graduated from Elim Bible College in New York.

Over the past twenty years, Jonathan has pastored in churches of forty to four thousand in Canada and the United States. He has planted a church, led as Executive Pastor, started non-profits, and served at a denominational level. He has personally discipled hundreds of new believers and trained leaders to become effective in discipleship.

Jonathan and his wife, Gina, are parents to two wonderful girls in Orlando, Florida.